Rethink Church

Rethink Church

Robert R. Davis

Rethink Church
© Copyright 2019, Robert R. Davis

Table of Contents

What is the Church   7

The Kingdom   17

The Name of Israel   29

Jesus the Messiah   39

Model of the Church   51

True Worship   57

Salvation   63

Church Leadership   71

The Sabbath   79

Tithes and Offerings   91

Spiritual Maturity   101

What God Wants   111

What is the Church?

We assume we know what the Church is because we see them everywhere, but those are merely the buildings. What does it really mean to be called the Church? To be more specific, what was Jesus referring to when He spoke of the Church?

Let's look at the scriptures, in order to have a foundation to build upon.

> *St. Matthew 16:13* **When Jesus came into the coasts of Caesarea Philippi, he asked his disciples, saying, Whom do men say that I the Son of man am?**
> *St. Matthew 16:14* *And they said, Some say that thou art John the Baptist: some, Elias; and others, Jeremias, or one of the prophets.*
> *St. Matthew 16:15* **He saith unto them, But whom say ye that I am?**
> *St. Matthew 16:16* **And Simon Peter answered and said, Thou art the Christ, the Son of the living God.**
> *St. Matthew 16:17* **And Jesus answered and said unto him, Blessed art thou, Simon Barjona: for flesh and blood hath not revealed it unto thee, but my Father which is in heaven.**
> *St. Matthew 16:18* **And I say also unto thee, That thou art Peter, and upon this rock I will build my Church; and the gates of hell shall not prevail against it.**

St. Matthew 16:19 And I will give unto thee the keys of the kingdom of heaven: and whatsoever thou shalt bind on earth shall be bound in heaven: and whatsoever thou shalt loose on earth shall be loosed in heaven.

St. Matthew chapter sixteen is the first time Jesus uses the term we have translated as Church. He said, "Upon this rock I will build my Church and the gates of hell shall not prevail against it."[1] In the original Greek, the word Jesus used was "Petra." This is close to the name Peter ("Petros") in Greek.

Most Catholic denominations agree that Peter is the rock. However, they differ on whom received the keys of the Kingdom.[2]

"In the Roman Catholic Church, Jesus' words are interpreted as the foundation of papacy infallibility and the continuous succession of popes.[3] The Eastern and Oriental Orthodox Churches reject the succession of popes and believe in the infallibility of the Church as a whole and not the Pope. They contend any individual regardless of their position is subject to error."[4] "Protestants on the other hand, reject the infallibility of the Church and its leaders. Instead they believe it signifies the Church will never be destroyed."[5]

We should look at this logically and scripturally to determine the true meaning. If Jesus is going to build His Church on this rock, whatever it is, the rock must be foundational. Is Peter the foundation of the Church? Is this even a biblical notion? There are no scriptures to support this assertion.

*Isaiah 28:16 **Therefore thus saith the Lord GOD, Behold, I lay in Zion for a foundation a stone, a tried stone, a precious corner stone, a sure foundation**: he that believeth shall not make haste.*

The book of Isaiah gives us clarity concerning the identification of the rock. The only foundation or stone God intended to build His Church on is the Messiah. How can Jesus both build the Church and be its cornerstone? To understand this we should look at Peter's declaration, which precedes Jesus' statement about the rock. "Thou art the Christ, the Son of the living God." (St. Matthew 16:16) Jesus built His Church upon this rock, which is the truth of Him being the Son of God, the Anointed One and the long prophesied Messiah.

Can the words Peter spoke really be consider a rock? Jesus said, flesh and blood did not reveal this truth to Peter, but His Father in heaven revealed it. Therefore, this is a truth of God, not Peter.

*St. Matthew 7:24 **Therefore whosoever heareth these sayings of mine, and doeth them**, I will liken him unto a wise man, which **built his house upon a rock**:*
*St. Matthew 7:25 And the rain descended, and the floods came, and the winds blew, and beat upon that house; and it fell not: **for it was founded upon a rock.***

Clearly, the Word of God is the true rock Jesus was referring to with His disciples. The Word or Truth of God is our sure foundation. Jesus is the Word become flesh, according to St. John 1:14. Therefore, He can be both the builder and foundation of the Church.

The next question we should ask is did Jesus intend to build a new religion (Christianity) upon the fact He is the Christ, the Son of the living God? In order to answer this question we first need to understand one of the prophecies concerning Him.

> *Acts 7:37 This is that **Moses**, which **said** unto the children of Israel, **A prophet shall the Lord your God raise up unto you of your brethren, like unto me;** him shall ye hear.*
> *Acts 7:38 **This is he, that was in the Church in the wilderness** with the angel which spake to him in the mount Sina [Sinai], and with our fathers: who received the lively oracles to give unto us:*

There was never a Church during the time of Moses, not as we understand the term. The word Church in the New Testament is "Ecclesia" in the original Greek. It means called out ones or assembly. Acts 7:37-38 is a quotation from Deuteronomy. Notice the original text does not read Church, but assembly.

> *Deuteronomy 18:15 **The LORD thy God will raise up unto thee a Prophet from the midst of thee, of thy brethren, like unto me;** unto him ye shall hearken;*
> *Deuteronomy 18:16 According to all that thou desiredst of the LORD thy God **in Horeb in the day of the assembly**, saying, Let me not hear again the voice of the LORD my God, neither let me see this great fire any more, that I die not.*
> *Deuteronomy 18:17 And the LORD said unto me, They have well spoken that which they have spoken.*

In the Old Testament, the term translated "Assembly" comes from the Hebrew word "Qahal", which means congregation, assembly or company. The root of the word means to gather or summon. The meaning of the Hebrew "Qahal" is almost identical to the Greek "Ecclesia."

Therefore, Jesus was not making a distinction between the Church and the congregation of Israel. The difference comes from how we translated the Hebrew versus the Greek words. Today, when we use the term, "Church" it automatically excludes the Jews (Israel). However, this was not the original intent of the expression. When the Church started it was almost completely Jewish.

We should look at the second and last time Jesus uses the term translated, "Church." It is also in the book of Matthew.

> *St. Matthew 18:15* ***Moreover if thy brother shall trespass against thee, go and tell him his fault between thee and him alone:*** *if he shall hear thee, thou hast gained thy brother.*
> *St. Matthew 18:16* ***But if he will not hear thee, then take with thee one or two more, that in the mouth of two or three witnesses every word may be established.***
> *St. Matthew 18:17* ***And if he shall neglect to hear them, tell it unto the Church: but if he neglect to hear the Church,*** *let him be unto thee as an heathen man and a publican.*

In this passage Jesus is talking about civil matters, not spiritual. This directive is for any disputes among God's people. Earlier in the book of Acts we saw Jesus was likened to Moses (the lawgiver). This passage shows Jesus acting in the same capacity as the prophet. Observe a similar procedure listed in Exodus.

Exodus 18:13 **And it came to pass on the morrow, that Moses sat to judge the people**: *and the people stood by Moses from the morning unto the evening.*

14 **And when Moses' father in law saw all that he did to the people, he said, What is this thing that thou doest to the people? why sittest thou thyself alone, and all the people stand by thee from morning unto even?**

15 And Moses said unto his father in law, Because the people come unto me to enquire of God:

16 When they have a matter, they come unto me; and I judge between one and another, and I do make them know the statutes of God, and his laws.

17 **And Moses' father in law said unto him, The thing that thou doest is not good.**

18 **Thou wilt surely wear away, both thou, and this people that is with thee: for this thing is too heavy for thee; thou art not able to perform it thyself alone.**

19 Hearken now unto my voice, I will give thee counsel, and God shall be with thee: Be thou for the people to God–ward, that thou mayest bring the causes unto God:

20 And thou shalt teach them ordinances and laws, and shalt shew them the way wherein they must walk, and the work that they must do.

21 **Moreover thou shalt provide out of all the people able men, such as fear God, men of truth, hating covetousness; and place such over them**, *to be rulers of thousands, and rulers of hundreds, rulers of fifties, and rulers of tens:*

22 **And let them judge the people at all seasons: and it shall be, that every great matter they shall bring unto thee, but every small matter they shall judge: so shall it be easier for thyself, and they shall bear the burden with thee.**

23 If thou shalt do this thing, and God command thee so, then thou shalt be able to endure, and all this people shall also go to their place in peace.

24 So Moses hearkened to the voice of his father in law, and did all that he had said.

25 And Moses chose able men out of all Israel, and made them heads over the people, rulers of thousands, rulers of hundreds, rulers of fifties, and rulers of tens.

*26 **And they judged the people at all seasons: the hard causes they brought unto Moses, but every small matter they judged themselves.***

Jesus simply refined the process Moses used with a three-step method for settling disputes. This reinforces His identity as being the prophet, like unto Moses (St. John 5:46).

1. Discuss the matter one on one
2. Bring one or two others (the witness of two or three)
3. Let the congregation (Church) decide the matter

We think of the Church as purely a spiritual entity. How could Jesus expect it to settle personal disputes? The answer is simple. He did not require a spiritual entity called the Church to handle these types of problems. These words were spoken to the Jews and they understood it pertained to the kingdom of Israel.

This directive is for His government, not the Church as we know it, but the Kingdom of God. The Church today is a result of the schism between the followers of the Law and the followers of Christ. It was not a construct of Jesus, due to the apostasy of Israel. He did not come to create a new religion (Christianity) or a different type of worship.

Remember, the Church was entirely Jewish in the beginning.

The Church is actually a fragmentation of Israel over the Cornerstone (Jesus) and His teachings. Christ never came to institute a Church. The term translated as "Church" is only mentioned twice in the Gospels. However, God's government, the Kingdom occurs over a hundred times. Jesus came to establish the Kingdom, not a Church.

> *Isaiah 9:6* **For unto us a child is born, unto us a son is given: and the government shall be upon his shoulder**: *and his name shall be called Wonderful, Counsellor, The mighty God, The everlasting Father, The Prince of Peace.*
> *Isaiah 9:7* **Of the increase of his government** *and peace there shall be no end, upon the throne of David, and* **upon his kingdom**, *to order it, and* **to establish it** *with judgment and with justice from henceforth even for ever. The zeal of the LORD of hosts will perform this.*

This scripture is generally accepted among Christians as pertaining to Jesus. It does not mention the Church, only the Kingdom (His government). The two entities were originally the same, but now they are vastly different. Today the Church is an organization of believers, designed for religious worship. In contrast, a kingdom is a monarchical form of government, designed to establish the rule of God in the lives of humanity.

The Church is a visible entity, but the Kingdom of God is not discernable to the human eye. The Church has members that can be counted. It can be seen and measured. However, the Kingdom is invisible and immeasurable.

*St. Luke 17:20 And when he was demanded of the Pharisees, when the kingdom of God should come, he answered them and said, **The kingdom of God cometh not with observation:***
*St. Luke 17:21 Neither shall they say, Lo here! or, lo there! for, **behold, the kingdom of God is within you.***

"Since the beginning of time, God's plan for humanity centered on the fact that God desired to have a personal relationship with mankind. It was never the Lord's plan to establish a religion. Religion is the human response to a deep spiritual vacuum in the recesses of our soul, for something we cannot describe or identify. For many, religion has been and continues to be a tireless preoccupation distracting them from the unresolved fears of the human heart. It is interesting to note that the Bible does not prescribe a formal method for worship or prayer."[6]

The Church as we know it today is an outgrowth of religion. There are about 34,000 different Christian groups in the world since AD 30. This is according to the World Christian Encyclopedia published in 2001. A denomination is a nicer word for divisions.

*1 Corinthians 3:3 **For ye are yet carnal: for whereas there is among you** envying, and strife, and **divisions, are ye not carnal**, and walk as men?*

Does this mean we should leave the Church? No, I am not advocating this at all. At the time of Jesus, Israel was anxiously awaiting the Kingdom of God. Let's look at the Kingdom a little closer to see God's true intention.

The Kingdom

St. Luke 13:18 Then said he, Unto what is the kingdom of God like? and whereunto shall I resemble it?

St. Luke 13:19 It is like a grain of mustard seed, which a man took, and cast into his garden; and it grew, and waxed a great tree; and the fowls of the air lodged in the branches of it.

St. Luke 13:20 And again he said, Whereunto shall I liken the kingdom of God?

St. Luke 13:21 It is like leaven, which a woman took and hid in three measures of meal, till the whole was leavened.

St. Luke 17:20 And when he was demanded of the Pharisees, when the kingdom of God should come, he answered them and said, The kingdom of God cometh not with observation:

St. Luke 17:21 Neither shall they say, Lo here! or, lo there! for, behold, the kingdom of God is within you.

"The book of Genesis opens with God creating the physical world. The precipice of His work was the creation of humans. Humanity was formed from God's very essence, the Holy Spirit. As His offspring, we are the gods of this world. The Creator appointed us to establish and implement the invisible Kingdom of Heaven in the visible earth. This is His purpose for creating mankind."[7]

When we think of the origins of the Kingdom of God, we normally think of Israel. However, Israel is a restorative act of God. Think about this, Jesus came to restore what we lost through the fall of Adam, not Israel. If Adam did not possess a Kingdom, how could Christ restore it?

Adam in the Bible is a Hebrew term meaning humanity. It includes both males and females. It is not a proper name in the book of Genesis. The term is sometimes translated as man and other times Adam, this leads us to believe there is a distinction, but there is not. The translators are attempting to clarify and make sense of the Hebrew text. In the first chapter of Genesis, the Hebrew "āḏām" was translated to man. In the garden story, chapters two and three, it becomes "Adam" a proper name, in contrast to the Woman. However, this is erroneous and leads us to wrong conclusions.

The Bible states, "God created man ("āḏām") in His own image, in the image of God created He him; male and female created He them (Genesis 1:26)." See how the text seamlessly goes from man and him, to male and female and them. If that is not enough proof, observe what Genesis chapter five has to say about the matter.

> *Genesis 5:2* **Male and female created he them**; *and blessed them,* **and called their name Adam,** *in the day* **when they were created***.*

God referred to both male and female as Adam. The scripture here is explicit. The author is going through great lengths to tell us Adam is an inclusive term meaning humanity or mankind. It is not a personal name for the first male, but rather a classification of the species. This should not be a controversial issue, but it is due to Eve.

Since the term Adam embodies male and female, then who is the Woman? We have been taught she is Adam's wife and therefore the term "āḏām" represents the male only, even though this disagrees with scripture, most accept this teaching. Genesis 2:23-24 cements the man wife ideology in our minds, because we use these verses in our marriage ceremonies. However, the apostle Paul declares this passage is a mystery.

When the Bible talks about something being a mystery, it is referring to a spiritual truth, which has been hidden somewhere in the scriptures.

> *Genesis 2:24 Therefore* ***shall a man leave his father and his mother, and shall cleave unto his wife: and they shall be one flesh.***

> *Ephesians 5:31 For this cause* ***shall a man leave his father and mother, and shall be joined unto his wife, and they two shall be one flesh.***
> *Ephesians 5:32* ***This is a great mystery:*** *but I speak* ***concerning Christ and the Church.***

Paul states this passage relates to Christ and the Church. How do Adam and the Woman relate to Christ and the Church and what is God concealing in the story?

In the book of Genesis, we have the first Adam in the garden and Paul tells us that Jesus is the last Adam (1 Corinthians 15:45-47). Since Christ is the last Adam, if we look closely at how they parallel we should be able clear up the mystery.

1. God causes Adam to sleep and opens his side
2. The Woman is formed from Adam
3. God presents the Woman to Adam as his bride

<u>God causes Adam to sleep and opens his side</u>
First, God causes Adam to fall into a deep sleep and then He opens up his side. What is the significance of this action? In the Bible, the term deep sleep is figurative of

19

death. By opening the side of Adam, God is symbolically taking the breath or life from him to create the Woman.

Most translations state God took one of Adam's ribs and made a woman. "However, according to Ziony Zevit, Distinguished Professor of Biblical Literature and Northwest Semitic Languages at American Jewish University in Bel-Air, California, "rib" is the wrong translation for '*tsela*' in the story of Adam and Eve. He believes that it should be translated as "a non-specific, general term," in other words, simply side."[8]

In parallel, God caused Jesus to fall into a deep sleep, which indicates His death on the cross. This was also the work of God. John states, "For God so loved the world that he gave his only begotten Son." After, Jesus the last Adam is in a deep sleep, His side is also opened.

> *St. John 19:33 But **when they came to Jesus, and saw that he was dead already**, they brake not his legs:*
> *St. John 19:34 But **one of the soldiers with a spear pierced his side**, and forthwith came there out blood and water.*

The blood is for the remission (canceling) of our sins and the water cleanses us. These are the components of the Spirit of God. By pouring out the blood and water from Jesus, God is symbolically taking the life from Him to create the Church.

The first Adam relates to the physical creation of the Woman. The last Adam correlates to the spiritual formation.

The Woman is formed from Adam

God creates the Woman from Adam. Remember, the bible declares, Adam is a term denoting both male and female. God creates the Woman, but she cannot be a literal female, since the gender already exists.

Think about this, would God command Adam to be fruitful and multiply (Genesis 1:28), without giving him the means to reproduce? That would be putting the cart before the horse, so to speak. Do we think God has dementia, of course not?

The Hebrew word "Asah" translated "Made" is used in the creation story for every living thing God created, except the formation of the Woman.

The Hebrew word "Banah" is used for the Woman, which means to build. This is the first time we see the word used in the Bible, the next place is Genesis 4:17 when Cain builds a city. The Woman is built, not made like the rest of creation.

> *Genesis 2:22 And the rib, which **the LORD God** had taken from man, **made [built] he a woman**, and brought her unto the man.*

To build means to form by ordering and uniting materials by gradual means into a composite whole. This means it took some time to form the Woman. It was not an instantaneous manifestation, which is why Adam needed to be in a deep sleep.

What did God build from Adam? The Woman represents a city. Since she is built from Adam prior to the original sin, the city is therefore holy. This is the original Holy City of God, long before Jerusalem. Can we prove this assumption? Yes, what is true of the first Adam must also be true of the last one.

This assumption if proved will turn our understanding of the garden event upside down. If the Woman is a city, then there were many people in the garden, when the serpent spoke. A detailed account is given, *In the Beginning: The Truth behind Genesis.*

Instead of a rib, blood and water came out of the last Adam, creating the Church. This entity was also built, not made.

> *St. Matthew 16:18 And I say also unto thee, That thou art Peter, and **upon this rock I will build my Church**; and the gates of hell shall not prevail against it.*

The building of the Church is also a gradual work. The Church was not presented to Jesus after His resurrection. It is still a future event. Concerning the Church the apostle Paul states, Jerusalem above is our mother (Galatians 4:22-26). This means, New Jerusalem is the city and the Church members represent the inhabitants. However, the two terms are interchangeable. Therefore, building the Church and building the city New Jerusalem are indistinguishable.

Jesus told His disciples that He was going away to prepare or build a place for them (St. John 14:2-3). The Woman He is building is New Jerusalem. There is a definite duality in Jesus' roles. As the last Adam He is still in a deep sleep, but as our Lord He is building His bride.

As I stated earlier, what is true of the first Adam must be true of the last. Therefore, since the Woman represents the Holy City with Jesus, the same must be true of the first

Adam. This is indeed a *Great Mystery*, as Paul has declared.

God presents the Woman to Adam as his bride

In the last point, after Adam is awakened God presents the Woman to him as his bride. Adam declares the Woman is bone of his bone and flesh of his flesh, meaning the two are one.

Subsequently, Adam renames the Woman and calls her Eve, because she is the mother of all living. Paul declares the same concerning the Church. He states, Jerusalem above is the mother of all of us.[9]

In parallel to the first Adam, New Jerusalem comes down from God out of heaven, prepared as a bride for Christ (Revelation 21:2). Jesus declares all who eat his flesh and drink his blood (communion) dwell in him and He dwells in them, meaning they are one (St. John 6:56). Later, he will write on all inhabitants of the Holy City the name of God, the name of city (New Jerusalem) and His new name. This effectively, renames the city. Just as the first Adam renamed his bride.

	First Adam	**Last Adam**
Taken from Adam's side	Bone and Flesh	Blood & Water
Woman formed from Adam	Physical	Spiritual
God presents bride to Adam	First Holy City (Eve)	Last Holy City (New Jerusalem)

We went through all of this to prove the Kingdom of God did not start with Israel, but Adam. Israel was part of the God's covenant to Abraham. All of the covenants after

23

Adam are restorative acts of God, to bring us back to our original intent.

Therefore, Adam did possess a Kingdom, via the Woman. This mystery has been hidden in the story of Adam and Eve for centuries. The rule of God in the hearts of humanity is the Kingdom of God.

The apostle Paul states in the book of Hebrews, "We are receiving a Kingdom that cannot be shaken."[10] How can we have the Kingdom inside and yet receive it as our inheritance later?

Remember, salvation, power and the Kingdom is a package deal. They are all bound tightly together. We receive salvation now, but we do not obtain the finalization until the judgment.

>*St. Matthew 24:13 But **he that** shall **endure unto the end, the same shall be saved.***

Think of it this way. You can go to a dealership and purchase a car today. Essentially the car is yours. You can keep it, drive it and even customize it, but if you do not fulfill your financial obligations to the lien holder, you can lose your rights to the automobile. Similarly, salvation and the Kingdom are yours now, but your actions can forfeit your privileges.

>*St. Luke 9:62 And **Jesus said** unto him, **No man, having put his hand to the plough, and looking back, is fit for the kingdom of God.***

If we endure until the end, we will inherit the Kingdom, which is New Jerusalem. This is paradise restored, where God dwells with humanity forever. There will be no Tree of Knowledge of good and evil, so there can be no chance of sin. The apostle Paul put it this way, "The sufferings of this present life are not worthy to be compared to be with the glory which shall be revealed in us."[11]

The Church and the Kingdom are supposed to be synonymous terms, but they are not. The Church has developed a system of rituals and rules designed to guarantee us God's favor. This is a yoke, which keeps us in bondage instead of giving us freedom.

> *St Matthew 23:1* **Then spake Jesus** *to the multitude, and to his disciples,*
> *St Matthew 23:2* **Saying, The scribes and the Pharisees sit in Moses' seat**: *St Matthew 23:3 All therefore whatsoever they bid you observe, that observe and do; but do not ye after their works: for they say, and do not.*
> *St Matthew 23:4* **For they bind heavy burdens and grievous to be borne, and lay them on men's shoulders**; *but they themselves will not move them with one of their fingers.*
> *St Matthew 23:5* **But all their works they do for to be seen of men**: *they make broad their phylacteries, and enlarge the borders of their garments,*
> *St Matthew 23:6 And* **[they] love the uppermost rooms at feasts, and the chief seats in the synagogues,**
> *St Matthew 23:7* **And greetings in the markets, and to be called of men, Rabbi**, *Rabbi.*

Jesus is describing the religious system of His day. Unfortunately, the Church today is to a large extent the same as Israel was in His time. However, this is not God's intention. Jesus said, "Come unto me all who labor and are heavy with burdens and He will give us rest."[12]

Am I advocating we leave the Church? Again no, God forbid. We still need to assemble, which is the meaning of the term Church. An assembly is a group of people gathered together in one place for a common purpose. Humans are by nature communal beings.

In the beginning God stated, "It is not good that the man should be alone; I will make him a help meet for him." We realize that the term translated in this scripture as man is actually the Hebrew word "ādām", which means male and female. It looks like God is saying it is not good for humans to be in isolation, we need community.

However, it is much more than that. The Woman was created to be a help meet for Adam (male and female). First we must understand there is no such thing as a "Helpmeet", which we render as "Helpmate" today. Helpmeet is not a word. The phrase is "help meet", which are two separate words. The word meet is archaic English term, meaning suitable, right or proper. However, the footnote from the original King James Version has a notation indicating the meaning in Hebrew was "as before him". This means the term meet actually has the connotation of face to face.

Let's take a closer look at the word help. In Hebrew the word is "Ezer". The meaning of this word is not simply help, but "succor". This is one who helps in times of hardship or distress. The Hebrew word is used 21 times in the Old Testament. Almost every instance of "Ezer" is used to describe God.

When we see the Lord is our help, we understand the term to mean a very strong help. "Ezer" was not intended to evoke images of docility, subservience or even equality.

Quite the opposite it carries the connotation of military might, power or an unstoppable force that is greater than the individual.

So, the help that was before (meet) Adam was the Holy City (Woman), in other words the Kingdom of God. The city that was built from Adam was meant to be a mighty power and advocate for humanity. This is why Jesus spoke of us saying, "We will do His works and even greater works." The greater works is what is carried out by the body of Christ or the government of God. Jesus could only do so much physically because of the limitations of time and space, but the Kingdom of God is virtually unlimited.

Christ carries the thought of an "Ezer" forward with the Holy Spirit. He said He would leave us the "Comforter", which is better translated Helper. Just as God in the Old Testament was our help in the times of hardship or distress; The Holy Ghost is our ever present Help today.

We have verified Jesus did not establish a new religion called the Church. He came to instigate the Kingdom of God within us. However, we still need to assemble ourselves together. To understand what God intended we need to look at the Church, before it fragmented. In other words, we need to look at Israel.

The Name of Israel

Genesis 32:24   And Jacob was left alone; and there wrestled a man with him until the breaking of the day.

Genesis 32:25   And when he saw that he prevailed not against him, he touched the hollow of his thigh; and the hollow of Jacob's thigh was out of joint, as he wrestled with him.

Genesis 32:26   And he said, Let me go, for the day breaketh. And he said, I will not let thee go, except thou bless me.

Genesis 32:27   And he said unto him, What *is* thy name? And he said, Jacob.

Genesis 32:28   And he said, Thy name shall be called no more Jacob, but Israel: for as a prince hast thou power with God and with men, and hast prevailed.

We already know Jesus did not intend to create a new religion, called Christianity. Israel on the other hand, was meant to be a physical representation of the Kingdom of God. As I said earlier, the kingdom of Israel was a restorative act. It was one of the steps in God's plan for the restoration of the human race.

The Kingdom was a spiritual reality to Adam and that is what Jesus restored. Israel was meant to be a physical pattern of the Kingdom of God. Physical archetypes are given in the Old Testament in order to help us understand the spiritual realities of the New Testament.

The Church is also a physical entity. If Jesus gave us the Church, then it doesn't match the pattern laid down in the Bible. The first Adam is natural and the last Adam (Jesus

Christ) is spiritual. Consequently, everything Christ gives us is spiritual.

> *1 Corinthians 15:44 It is sown a natural body; it is raised a spiritual body. **There is a natural body, and there is a spiritual body.***
> *1 Corinthians 15:45 And so it is written, The first man Adam was made a living soul; the last Adam was made a quickening spirit.*
> *1 Corinthians 15:46 **Howbeit that was not first which is spiritual, but that which is natural; and afterward that which is spiritual.***
> *1 Corinthians 15:47 **The first man** is of the **earth**, earthy: **the second man** is the Lord from **heaven.***

Furthermore, the scope of the Church is less than Israel's. The primary focus of the Church today is the worship of God, but the focus of ancient Israel was also the government of God. Worship covers religious acts, but government encompasses every aspect of human life.

The Kingdom comprises the government and worship of God. However, things are regulated and divided into Church (religion) and State (government). There is no such separation in the Kingdom of God. Therefore, Israel is our prototype to understand God's plan, not today's Church.

Ancient Israel is our physical model for the government of God. It should serve as our blueprint or example for understanding the spiritual Kingdom. Consequently, we need to take a closer look at Israel.

Jacob wrestled with God and asked for a blessing.[13] The only thing he was given was a name change, to Israel. How is this act a blessing?

The name Jacob means "one who grabs the heel." It represents someone who trips up another, a supplanter or deceiver. However, today the Hebrew meaning of the name Israel is not clear.

"In Genesis 32:28, the form לאִרשׂי (Israel) appears to be a compilation of two elements. The first one is the noun לא (El), the common abbreviation of Elohim, meaning God. The second part of the name appears to be related to the verb הרשׂ I (Sara I), the meaning is uncertain and explained in many ways, chiefly because it is limited to contexts which discuss the struggle of Jacob with the Angel of YHWH (Genesis 32:29 and Hosea 12:4 only), insinuating that where the language uses the common verb *struggle*, the Hebrew uses a word that is specifically reserved for a certain action: the action of struggling with God."[14]

*Genesis 32:28 And he said, **Thy name shall be called no more Jacob, but Israel**: for as a prince hast **thou power with God and with men, and hast prevailed.***

"However, even though Genesis 32:28 uses the enigmatic verb רשׂי —which is assumed to mean to struggle, it could mean something else entirely. It is by no means certain that this verb is etymologically linked to the name Israel. When I say, "I named him Bob because that seemed like a good idea," I certainly do not mean to say that the name Bob means "good idea." [15]

Let's breakup the name Israel (ישׂראל) into its parts, the first part is "Isra" (רשׂי) and the second is "El" (לא). Note Hebrew word construction is reversed from English. The most likely meaning for the first part of the name is the verb "Yashar" (רשׂי), meaning upright.

The main reason certain Hebrew words are unclear today is because the orthography used throughout the years has continually changed.

> *Orthography is a set of conventions for how to write a language. It includes rules of spelling, hyphenation, capitalization, word breaks, emphasis, and punctuation.*

If our theory is correct, the name Israel would mean "Upright of God" or "Righteous of God", not "Who prevails with God".

This makes more sense on a purely logically level. This name change would indeed be a blessing. Jacob means deceiver and every time someone called his name that is what he heard. He naturally lived up to his name. Now when he hears Israel (Righteous of God), it forms a new identity for him. We know it worked because we know the end of the story.

The purpose of Jacob wrestling until he was blessed, is a pictorial representation of faith in action. The apostle Paul put it this way, "Fight the good fight of faith."[16]

Jacob already had the blessings of God before he wrestled with God. This was evident in his life. However, he was desperate for the Lord to allow him to return home in peace (Genesis 28:21).

> *Genesis 27:36 And he said, **Is not he rightly named Jacob?** for he hath supplanted me these two times: **he took away my birthright; and, behold, now he hath taken away my blessing.** And he said, Hast thou not reserved a blessing for me?*

*Genesis 27:41 **And Esau hated Jacob** because of the blessing wherewith his father blessed him: **and Esau said in his heart**, The days of mourning for my father are at hand; then will **I slay my brother Jacob.***

If the meaning of Israel was really he "Who prevails with God", then why should he fear his brother? If he can fight with God and win, he should be able to defeat Esau.

Even, after the name change Israel greatly feared his brother. This is because even though God changed his name, Esau did not know about it. For that reason, he presented Esau with gifts and humbled himself before his brother. This type of restoration is in line with what God requires when someone steals or causes loss to another.

Leviticus 6:1 And the LORD spake unto Moses, saying,
*Leviticus 6:2 **If a soul sin**, and commit a trespass against the LORD, and lie unto his neighbour in that which was delivered him to keep, or in fellowship, or in a thing taken away by violence, or hath deceived his neighbour;*
*Leviticus 6:3 Or have found that which was lost, and **lieth concerning it, and sweareth falsely; in any of all these that a man doeth, sinning therein:***
*Leviticus 6:4 Then it shall be, because he hath sinned, and is guilty, that he shall restore that which he took violently away, or **the thing which he hath deceitfully gotten**, or that which was delivered him to keep, or the lost thing which he found,*
*Leviticus 6:5 Or all that about which he hath sworn falsely; **he shall even restore it in the principal, and shall add the fifth part more thereto, and give***

it unto him to whom it appertaineth*, in the day of his trespass offering.*

Jacob made restitution to Esau his brother whom he deceived, which was in line with the Law, long before it was written. Now, we can see Jacob (the deceiver) has truly become Israel (the righteous of God).

This gives fresh meaning to the name Israel. We know Jesus is the King of Israel, but now it means King of Righteousness. This agrees with the Apostle Paul's assertion that Jesus is a priest after the order of Melchizedek, which means king of righteousness.

In addition, this definition of Israel agrees with another appellation for the nation, "Jeshurun." "This is a poetic name for Israel, used as a token of affection, meaning "Upright One." This name shows that before the Masoretic pronunciation aids were added, the letters שׁ and שׂ were once the same: יְשֻׁרוּן (Jeshurun) or יִשְׂרָאֵל (Israel)."[17] This means the root word is identical for both names, "Yashar" (Upright or Righteous).

Here is why the name is important and why we took so much time trying to derive its true meaning. The name's meaning shows all believers are included in Israel. Every believer is the righteousness of God. We are all the children of Israel, which means we are all included in the blessings. This is revealed through the meaning of the name of Israel. Paul also declares the same by saying; we are the seed of Abraham through faith and as the body of Christ.

The true meaning of the name Israel indicates it was always meant to be a multinational kingdom. This is why God told

Abraham through his seed all nations of the earth would be blessed.[18]

Unfortunately, the term Jew has replaced or become synonymous with Israel. When we hear the expression, "Jew" we automatically think of the religion, Judaism. It was never God's intention to convert the world to Judaism. The Lord's desire is for everyone to be a part of His Kingdom, Israel. This is one reason why there is no prescribed method for prayer or worship.

When I speak of believers being Israel, I mean spiritual Israel. We are part of the invisible Kingdom of God. Our physical example of the Kingdom is ancient Israel, which should not be confused with the current nation of Israel.

> *Isaiah 44:5* ***One shall say, I am the LORD'S; and another shall*** *call himself by the name of Jacob; and another shall subscribe with his hand unto the LORD, and* ***surname himself by the name of Israel.***

When people think of Israel and the Kingdom of God, they naturally think of a monarchy. Our minds go to King David and Solomon as leaders of God's people, but Israel did not start out as a monarchy.

Ancient Israel was originally a theocracy, which is a form of government where a deity is the supreme civil ruler and ecclesiastical authorities interpret the laws. In the Bible, this was the time of the Judges of Israel. However, this form of government soon gave way to a monarchial rule, because of the people's discontent with Samuel's sons.

> *1 Samuel 8:11 And he said,* ***This will be the manner of the king that shall reign over you: He***

will take your sons, and appoint them for himself,
for his chariots, and to be his horsemen; and some
shall run before his chariots.
1 Samuel 8:12 And he will appoint him captains
over thousands, and captains over fifties; and will
set them to ear his ground, and to reap his harvest,
and to make his instruments of war, and instruments
of his chariots.
*1 Samuel 8:13 **And he will take your daughters to***
be confectionaries, and to be cooks, and to be
bakers.
*1 Samuel 8:14 **And he will take your fields, and***
your vineyards, and your oliveyards, even the best
of them, and give them to his servants.
*1 Samuel 8:15 **And he will take the tenth of your***
***seed,** and of your vineyards, and give to his officers,*
and to his servants.
*1 Samuel 8:16 **And he will take your menservants,***
***and your maidservants,** and your goodliest young*
men, and your asses, and put to his work.
*1 Samuel 8:17 **He will take the tenth of your sheep:***
and ye shall be his servants.
1 Samuel 8:18 And ye shall cry out in that day
because of your king which ye shall have chosen
you; and the LORD will not hear you in that day.
*1 Samuel 8:19 **Nevertheless the people refused to***
obey the voice of Samuel; and they said, Nay; but
we will have a king over us;
*1 Samuel 8:20 **That we also may be like all the***
***nations;** and that our king may judge us, and go out*
before us, and fight our battles.

It is clear from the scripture a monarchy was not God's
desire for Israel. Therefore, we should envision the
Kingdom as a theocracy. A monarchy is a government
where an individual inherits the role of sovereign and

bequeaths it to their heir. This type of government was the norm in ancient times, but has since fallen out of favor. This is in part because this form of government is very prone to corruption and abuse. In fact, God warned the people before they changed their form of governance.

In both types of government, leaders are prone to corruption. Yet, there is a big difference between the two. In First Samuel chapter eight, the elders of Israel had the freedom to gather and complain to Samuel about his advanced age and sons' behavior and asked for a king. The request upset Samuel and he went to God in prayer.[19] However, in a monarchy a group of elders would never complain about a king's age or his sons. If you upset a king, the result would be certain death.

A king exerts absolute power, but a judge does not. The people had the freedom to voice grievances against judges, but kings are supreme rulers. Although it is impossible to eliminate corruption in government, the theocracy system of judges gives the people a voice.

Moses was Israel's first judge. He was also, their lawgiver and a prophet. Yet, the people constantly complained to and against him. Do not get me wrong, it has never been proper to fight against God's leadership. On the other hand, the Kingdom of God was never intended to give leaders absolute power. The only sovereign was and is God. Is your Church run more like a theocracy or a monarchy? As you rethink Church, it is just one more thing to ponder.

Jesus the Messiah

Isaiah 9:6 For unto us a child is born, unto us a son is given: and the government shall be upon his shoulder: and his name shall be called Wonderful, Counsellor, The mighty God, The everlasting Father, The Prince of Peace.
Isaiah 9:7 Of the increase of his government and peace there shall be no end, upon the throne of David, and upon his kingdom, to order it, and to establish it with judgment and with justice from henceforth even forever. The zeal of the LORD of hosts will perform this.

As we have already seen, Jesus is not the initiator of a new religion, but of a new government called the Kingdom of God. He is the King of Israel, which means the righteous of God. However, Christ never came to reign over the physical nation of Israel, but over the spiritual one.

The Messiah is supposed to sit on the throne of David in order to establish Israel with judgment and justice, according to Isaiah chapter nine. If Jesus is the anointed one of God, then He must meet certain criteria.

- He must be an Israelite (now called Jewish)
- He must be from the tribe of Judah
- He must be a descendant both of David and Solomon
- He must rebuild the temple
- He must bring peace

Jesus as the Messiah is a stumbling stone, which has tripped up the Jews for centuries. According to Hebrew law, to determine whether a person is Jewish or not, depends solely on their parents. If both parents are Jewish, their child is Jewish. If one of the parents is not Jewish, the ethnicity of the mother passes down to the child.

No one disputes the Jewishness of Mary. According to scriptures Joseph is not the biological father of Jesus and we know God is not an Israelite. However, Jesus meets the first criteria through His mother. He is Jewish (Deuteronomy 17:15).

The second condition is Jesus must be from the tribe of Judah. This derives from the book of Genesis.

> *Genesis 49:10* ***The sceptre shall not depart from Judah, nor a lawgiver from between his feet, until Shiloh come;*** *and unto him shall the gathering of the people be.*

The Hebrew word "Shebet" has been interpreted as scepter, but it is normally translated to the word "Rod." There is no historical record of any king of Israel or Judah having a scepter. Historically, kings use scepters, but rods are the tools of shepherds. The difference is significant. Scepters are ornamental, while rods are practical.

The rod was an instrument used to defend the weak sheep by beating off their enemies—eagles, snakes, wild animals, mountain lions, bears and more. It could be thrown like a spear. The rod is an instrument used for correction, to stop a pattern of behavior. Spiritually speaking the rod is the Word of God.

Consequently, Genesis 49:10 means the Word (Law) and someone who declares the Law (priests, prophets and the like) will not disappear from Judah until the Messiah (Shiloh) arrives. How does this apply to Judah?

Jerusalem the Holy city of God was located in the territory of Judah (technically Benjamin) and in the kingdom of Judah after Israel split. Benjamin and Judah are linked together and after David captured the city, the border ran through the middle of the city and temple. When Israel split, the tribes of Benjamin and Judah were considered one tribe.[20]

Jerusalem is the Holy City of God. According to scriptures, it is where God dwells and subsequently where His Word abides. It was the central location where the priests and Levites functioned. This city is where God gives His people rest forever.[21]

According to Genesis 49:10 the law and the priests will not cease from Jerusalem, until the Messiah comes in bodily form. Shortly, after the death of Jesus the temple was destroyed and has not been rebuilt to date. This is a physical sign that the scepter (rod) has departed from Judah. There is no one other than Jesus who would fill the second criteria before the destruction of the temple in 70 A.D.

The third condition is Jesus must be a descendant of both David and Solomon. In order to prove Jesus is a descendant of David, genealogies must be used.

Joseph's genealogy points to him being from the tribe of Judah.[22] However, Joseph is reputedly not the biological father of Jesus, so it does not count.[23] According to Hebrew law, a child cannot inherit tribal lineage through adoption. This invalidates the genealogy of St. Matthew from pertaining to Jesus as the Messiah.

However, another genealogy appears in the book of St. Luke. This list of relatives is different from the book of Matthew. The traditional reason for this discrepancy is the lineage belongs to Mary, not Joseph. Although the mother determines who is Jewish and who is not. It is the father's heritage that governs your vocation. Kingship like the priesthood must come through the father's lineage. Since an adopted son cannot inherit tribal lineage, they are incapable of being priests or kings.

If this is Mary's genealogy, it cannot be used to determine if Jesus can be king. In addition, the lineage connects us to David through Nathan, not Solomon. This bloodline is invalid because Nathan was never king. Therefore, his descendants cannot inherit the crown.

Clearly, Jesus is not a descendant of David and Solomon. Therefore, He cannot inherit the throne and sit as king over Israel. This may come as a shock to Christians, but Jews already know this fact. It is one of the main reasons used to reject Jesus as the Messiah. He has become a stumbling block to them in accepting what God has provided.

Jews and Christians seem to agree the Messiah will be of the lineage of David, but Jesus does not meet this criterion. Yet, Jesus is Shiloh.

How can Jesus be the Christ and not be a descendant of David and Solomon? This is a problem of selective vision. We see the scripture where God promises Solomon to establish his throne forever (1 Kings 9:5). However, we fail to notice the promise to David and Solomon is conditional.

*1 Kings 2:4 And **if thou wilt walk before me, as David thy father walked, in integrity of heart, and***

in uprightness, to do according to all that I have commanded thee, and wilt keep my statutes and my judgments:
1 Kings 2:5 Then I will establish the throne of thy kingdom upon Israel for ever, as I promised to David thy father, saying, There shall not fail thee a man upon the throne of Israel.
1 Kings 2:6 But if ye shall at all turn from following me, ye or your children, and will not keep my commandments and my statutes which I have set before you, but go and serve other gods, and worship them:
1 Kings 2:7 Then will I cut off Israel out of the land which I have given them; and this house, which I have hallowed for my name, will I cast out of my sight; and Israel shall be a proverb and a byword among all people:

This promise is repeated in the book of Chronicles. The wording is slightly different, but the meaning is undeniably the same.

2 Chronicles 7:17 And as for thee, if thou wilt walk before me, as David thy father walked, and do according to all that I have commanded thee, and shalt observe my statutes and my judgments;
2 Chronicles 7:18 Then will I stablish the throne of thy kingdom, according as I have covenanted with David thy father, saying, There shall not fail thee a man to be ruler in Israel.
2 Chronicles 7:19 But if ye turn away, and forsake my statutes and my commandments, which I have set before you, and shall go and serve other gods, and worship them;
2 Chronicles 7:20 Then will I pluck them up by the roots out of my land which I have given them;

43

and this house, which I have sanctified for my name, will I cast out of my sight, and will make it to be a proverb and a byword among all nations.

Clearly, the promise of David's descendant sitting on the throne is conditional. We know from the scriptures that Israel turned from God. He kept His Word by removing them from the land and casting the temple (house) out of His sight.

Since the Jews were removed from their land and the temple destroyed, the conditional prophecy and promise of David's heir sitting on the throne has been nullified. The question becomes how does the Messiah still relate to David?

The prophecies to David were conditional. However, Isaiah gives us an unconditional prophecy concerning the Messiah.

*Isaiah 11:1 And **there shall come forth a rod out of the stem of Jesse**, and a Branch shall grow out of his roots:*

David is the son of Jesse. So, it is logical to connect this unconditional prophecy with his conditional message from God. However, after the conditions promised to David were broken, then we must look only at the unconditional promise of Isaiah.

The scripture speaks of Jesse, but there are still a myriad of references to David. However, the Messiah is no longer required to be a descendant of Solomon, after the apostasy of Israel.

Therefore, if the genealogy in the book of St. Luke belongs to Mary, the lineage of Jesus does entitle him to be the Messiah. The bloodline of Jesse, not Solomon is the qualification.

Jesus is called the root, offspring, seed and son of David. At times, He is even called David. The name David means "Beloved," Jesus is the ultimate beloved of God (St. Mark 1:11).

What is the real relationship between David and Jesus? David is an archetype for the Messiah. We see the same literary device used with John the Baptist. Elijah serves as the prototype for John's ministry. Jesus declared John was Elijah the prophet, which was prophesied to return before the Messiah.[24] John the Baptist was not a literal reincarnation of the prophet Elijah. We are supposed to see the similitude between them. The same holds true for David and Jesus.

How is David the prototype of Jesus? David did not inherit the crown from Saul. He did not have the proper bloodline to be king of Israel. David was chosen directly by God to be king of Israel. Likewise, Jesus does not have the proper bloodline to be king (via Solomon), but God chose him (St. Matthew 12:18). David was the least among his brethren, so was Jesus (St. John 1:45-46).

Let's look closer at the parallels between David and Jesus. The prophet Samuel was told not to look on the outward appearance when looking for the anointed, because the Lord looks at the heart. The same held true for Jesus (Isaiah 53:2-3). Samuel in this instance represents the religious leaders of Israel.

After Samuel anointed David, King Saul tried several times to kill him. Likewise, after the Spirit anointed Jesus there were attempts on Jesus' life (St. John 10:31-39, St. Luke 4:28-30). In this instance, Saul represents the religious leaders of Israel.

Clearly, Jesus is the seed and archetype of David. A literal descendant of David and Solomon to the throne is impossible due to the sins of Israel. The removal of the temple only reinforces this fact. Israel has nullified the third criteria. However, Jesus is truly the beloved.

The fourth condition is Jesus must rebuild the temple. This relates to the second criteria. The Messiah must restore the temple because after Shiloh appears the rod and lawgiver (temple) are removed from Judah.

The temple is always located within the kingdom. Where is Jesus' Kingdom?

> *St. Luke 17:20 And **when he was demanded of the Pharisees, when the kingdom of God should come, he answered them and said, The kingdom of God cometh not with observation:***
> *St. Luke 17:21 Neither shall they say, Lo here! or, lo there! for, **behold, the kingdom of God is within you.***

The Kingdom of God is spiritual, not physical. Therefore, the temple is also spiritual. This means the rod (Law) and lawgiver are now located inside of us.

> *Jeremiah 31:33 But **this shall be the covenant that I will make with the house of Israel;** After those days, saith the LORD, **I will put my law in their***

inward parts, and write it in their hearts; and will be their God, and they shall be my people.
Jeremiah 31:34 And they shall teach no more every man his neighbour, and every man his brother, saying, Know the LORD: for they shall all know me, from the least of them unto the greatest of them, saith the LORD: for I will forgive their iniquity, and I will remember their sin no more.

The Holy Spirit serves as both the Law and the lawgiver, dwelling in our temples (bodies). All of this well and good, but the Messiah must build the temple. How does this apply to Jesus?

Jesus said, "Destroy this temple that is made with hands and within three days I will build another made without hands."[25] This is the work of the Spirit of God. This is why the scriptures declare Jesus will baptize with the Holy Ghost.[26] Jesus fulfills yet another criterion. By giving us the Spirit, He is in reality building the temple or dwelling place of God inside of us.

John declares, Jesus will baptize with the Holy Ghost, but where in the Bible do we see this happening?

On the physical side we see it in St John 20:22. This act mimics Genesis 2:7, where God breathed into the nostrils of humankind.

On the spiritual side we see it in Revelation chapter eight. Where we see an angel holding a golden censer and he offers it upon the altar of God with incense and the prayers of the saints. This offering is a sweet aroma or pleasant fragrance before the Lord.

"The angel, who is fulfilling the role of a priest, takes the censer fills it with fire from the altar and casts it to the earth. Most commentaries relate this seal to the anger of God, because the censer is thrown to the earth. However, notice the censer of fire being thrown to the earth is the same one used to offer up the prayers of the saints. This indicates the act was an answer to the prayers of the saints.

In Revelation chapter eight we see the angel throwing the fire from the altar down to earth. In Acts chapter two we see the fire falling on the 120 in the upper room. Both of these scriptures are describing the day of Pentecost.

The angel, who we see functioning in the role of a priest, can only be Jesus Christ, our high priest. How do we know this is true? The scriptures state only Christ will baptize us with the Holy Ghost and fire. (St. Matthew 3:11, St. Luke 3:16) Why would Jesus be depicted as an angel, when He is the Messiah?

An angel is a messenger of God and Christ is the messenger of the New Covenant."[27]

> *Malachi 3:1 Behold, I will send my messenger, and he shall prepare the way before me: and **the Lord, whom ye seek**, shall suddenly come to his temple, **even the messenger of the covenant**, whom ye delight in: behold, he shall come, saith the LORD of hosts.*

Therefore, it is Jesus who builds the temple of God within us via the Spirit of God. We saw two witnesses of this fact, one physical and the other spiritual.

The fifth and last condition is Jesus must bring peace to the kingdom or Israel (the Righteous of God).

Since the kingdom and the temple are inside of us. The peace that Jesus gives must also be internal.

> *St. John 14:27* ***Peace I leave with you, my peace I give unto you:*** *not as the world giveth, give I unto you.* ***Let not your heart be troubled, neither let it be afraid.***

The peace Christ gives us is not the absence of conflict, but of fear. As with all things that pertain to Christ there is a duality. The spiritual fulfillment is now and the physical is after the judgment.

The Kingdom is a multinational entity. Through it, Christ has brought peace to the world. Therefore, Jesus has fulfilled the last criteria. This shows Jesus is truly the Christ.

Jesus did not the initiate Christianity, but the Kingdom of God. He is the true King of Israel, which means the righteous of God. However, Christ never came to reign over the physical nation of Israel, but over the spiritual one. He sits on the throne, selected by God like David in order to establish judgment and justice in our hearts.

Jesus and everything connected to Him is internal or spiritual. Why then do we give so much time, energy and importance to our religious external rituals? We know God does not exist in buildings, but we sure act as if He does. Our whole demeanor changes when we get to our Church, synagogue or mosque. Those places are not holy, our bodies, souls and spirits are the true holy places of God. In a sense, we have all tripped over the stumbling block of Jesus as the Messiah.

Model of the Church

Romans 11:17 And if some of the branches be broken off, and thou, being a wild olive tree, wert graffed in among them, and with them partakest of the root and fatness of the olive tree;

We are all included in Israel, not Judaism. This is what the apostle Paul was alluding to when he spoke of the good olive tree.

The good olive tree is a symbol of Israel. The branches are the people or children of Israel. Notice all of the branches were not broken off, just some of them. The wild olive tree represents the Gentiles. The Gentiles are grafted into Israel and partake of the root and fatness of the tree. Jesus is the root of the tree, which means He is the source of nourishment. Fatness in the Bible denotes productively and fertileness, which are the blessings of God. This grafting is spiritual not natural.

If the term Israel really stands for the Righteous of God, then it makes sense that it includes all people.

> *Galatians 3:14* ***That the blessing of Abraham might come on the Gentiles through Jesus Christ;*** *that we might receive the promise of the Spirit through faith.*

> *Galatians 3:26 For ye **are all the children of God** by faith in Christ Jesus.*
> *Galatians 3:27 For as many of you as have been baptized into Christ have put on Christ.*

Galatians 3:28 **There is neither Jew nor Greek, there is neither bond nor free, there is neither male nor female: for ye are all one in Christ Jesus.** *Galatians 3:29 And if ye be Christ's, then are ye Abraham's seed, and heirs according to the promise.*

The promises and blessing were made to Abraham and we are included through Jesus Christ. We have been spiritually grafted into Israel.

I think it may help if we separate Judaism from Israel. The promises given to Abraham, Isaac and Israel (Jacob) were before the Law. The Law and its rituals came later. The Lord promised to be a God to Abraham and his seed. Israel is the seed. Judaism could be thought of as the mechanism to instruct Israel in the ways of God. The apostle Paul puts it this way, "the Law was our schoolmaster until Christ. Now that Jesus has come we no longer needed a schoolmaster."[28]

The Law with its rituals, traditions and all of the outer ceremonies are no longer needed, according to Paul. So, why are we carrying all of this forward through the Church?

Since we no longer need a schoolmaster, are we now without any law? Can we just do whatever we feel is right?

St. John 13:34 **A new commandment I give unto you, That ye love one another; as I have loved you,** *that ye also love one another.*
St. John 13:35 **By this shall all men know that ye are my disciples**, *if ye have love one to another.*

This Law has been written upon the tablets of our hearts by the Spirit of God. This is another allusion of Jesus being a prophet just like Moses, who had the Law written upon tablets of stone by the finger of God.

Everything that Jesus has given us is spiritual. Nothing He has done is for the external self. The gifts of salvation and the Spirit, the new Law and even our worship is spiritual not physical.

So, where did we get our model for the Church? To answer this question we need to understand the Apostle John's vision of the two beasts in Revelation 13. The first beast out of the sea with seven heads and ten horns represents human government. The second beast out of the earth looks like a lamb, but speaks like a dragon symbolizes world religion. If you want the details of how I came to those conclusions, then read "The Final Message – Understanding the Book of Revelation."

The second beast, which is religion, causes the people to create an image. Anyone who refuses to worship the created image will be killed.[29] Okay, how can the second beast cause people to construct an image and then force them to worship it? Isn't the second beast the antichrist that will have the power to mesmerize people to do his bidding?

The second beast deceives many because he looks like a lamb (Christ), but he speaks as a dragon (Satan). Many today are still looking for a literal person to appear as the antichrist. This thinking has allowed the false prophet to establish himself almost unnoticed.

Let's clear this up by defining a few things. The image made by the second beast via the people, was created in the image of the first. This means the image will have the characteristics of the first creature. This beast represents human government, as I stated earlier. So, what government does the first beast exemplify? We are looking at the sixth head of the first beast in Revelation 13. This represents the Roman Empire. The second beast also known as the false prophet (religion) causes the people (citizens of the empire) to erect an image to Rome that will be worshipped. The image the people built was the Church. This answers the question of how the second beast can cause the people to construct an image and then force them to worship it.

History bears out people who refused to worship the Church were killed. During the Inquisition the Church executed people in an effort to combat heresy. Since we are looking at the government of the Roman Empire (6th Head), the image that was constructed is the Roman Catholic Church.

> *Disclaimer: This information should not cause us to condemn the Catholic Church, but it should induce us pray for it.*

If we fast forward in the book of Revelation to chapter seventeen, we see the Church is called the mother of harlots and abominations of the earth. This means, the Church has reproduced itself and subsequently its practices. Namely, we (the Church) have emulated all of the rituals, traditions and outward ceremonies that Paul said we no longer needed.

Here's the real problem. Religion (2nd Beast) has caused people to create the Church in the image of government (1st Beast).

*Romans 8:29 For whom he did foreknow, he also did predestinate **to be conformed to the image of his Son**, that he might be the firstborn among many brethren.*

The true assembly of believers, which is spiritual Israel, must be created in the image of Christ.

So, what is the solution? Is reformation the answer? There are always movements afoot to reform the Church, but they will not work. A quick look at history will show we have gone to various periods of reformation. It has been said the definition of insanity is doing the same thing over and over again and expecting different results.

Think of it this way, if you try on a pair of shoes that are one size too small and you return them to the clerk, does he add more leather and rubber to make them fit? Of course not, he brings you a new pair in your size. They will look exactly the same. However, you know the difference immediately, once you put them on your feet.

Similarly, instead of trying to reform Church, we should rethink it and create it anew. We will have the same buildings, so they will look the same. But, what goes on inside the buildings will feel totally different.

We need to transform the Church into the image of the firstborn, which is Christ. So, let's turn our attention to what it should look like on the inside.

True Worship

St. John 4:21 Jesus saith unto her, Woman, believe me, the hour cometh, when ye shall neither in this mountain, nor yet at Jerusalem, worship the Father.
St. John 4:22 Ye worship ye know not what: we know what we worship: for salvation is of the Jews.
St. John 4:23 But the hour cometh, and now is, when the true worshippers shall worship the Father in spirit and in truth: for the Father seeketh such to worship him.
St. John 4:24 God is a Spirit: and they that worship him must worship him in spirit and in truth.

What is Jesus saying in this text? Worship of God will no longer be confined to a specific place, the temple in Jerusalem. The spiritual reality was replacing the physical example. Christ revealed that the true worshipers will worship God in Spirit and Truth.

First, what does it mean to worship God? Worship is an act of reverence or devotion to the Lord. Every religion has a form of worship they deem acceptable in their gatherings. However, we want to know what God considers acceptable.

What does it mean to worship God in Spirit and in Truth? This question elicits as many different answers as we have Churches. Therefore, we should carefully search the scriptures for the correct answer.

Let's try to decipher what truth is before we delve into worship. What does the Bible define as truth? Thankfully, Jesus tells us, "The Word of God is Truth."[30] So, what does it mean to worship God in the Word (Truth)? We

57

show reverence to the Lord by obeying or following His Word.

> *Proverbs 21:3* **To do justice and judgment is more acceptable to the LORD than sacrifice.**

> *1 Samuel 15:22 And Samuel said, Hath the LORD as great delight in burnt offerings and sacrifices, as in* **obeying the voice of the LORD? Behold, to obey is better than sacrifice, and to hearken than the fat of rams.**

God is no more satisfied with our worship in Church services than He was with the multitude of animal sacrifices the Jews offered Him. They are both ceremonial external forms of appeasement. The Father does not need to be placated. He is a loving God, not an angry one. Obedience to His Word is the true form of worship the Lord desires of us.

Jesus said, "Do not be without understanding, external things do not defile us."[31] The opposite is also true, ritualistic practices cannot make us righteous. Never put form over substance. Holding our hands up in a service is meaningless without obedience to God's Word.

Now that we know what it means to worship in Truth, what does it means to worship in the Spirit? It is not as mystically as it sounds or people make it out to be. We only need to understand the role of the Holy Ghost to see the connection.

> *St. John 16:12* **I have yet many things to say unto you, but ye cannot bear them now.**
> *St. John 16:13* **Howbeit when he, the Spirit of truth, is come, he will guide you into all truth:** *for*

*he shall not speak of himself; but **whatsoever he shall hear, that shall he speak: and he will shew you things to come.***
*St. John 16:14 He shall glorify me: for **he shall receive of mine, and shall shew it unto you.***
*St. John 16:15 **All things that the Father hath are mine:** therefore said I, that **he shall take of mine, and shall shew it unto you.***

We worship God in Truth by obeying the Word. However, the written Word is finite. By that, I mean we are not continually writing more scriptures. We do not make additions to the Bible, what is written is written. Although the scriptures are holy, they do not address everything there is in life. Therefore, we need the Holy Spirit to fill in the gaps and to give us understanding.

The Holy Ghost is also called the Spirit of Truth and we know God's Word is Truth.[32] We must obey the Spirit, as well as the written Word. This is what it means to worship in Spirit and in Truth.

For example, the apostle Paul was well versed in the scriptures and customs of the Hebrews. He was a Pharisee. There was a prohibition against eating meat (food) offered to idols. He knew there was no such thing as an idol, because there is only one God. Therefore, Paul could eat anything sold in the markets, as long as he gave thanks to God for it. However, he also knew some believers did not have the same knowledge and would stumble on this point. Paul concluded, "If eating meat causes my brother to sin (offends) then I will no longer eat it."[33]

Where did Paul get this knowledge concerning idols? How did he obtain the wisdom, not to use his freedom to eat meat? This is the role and purpose of the Holy Spirit. How did this play out in Paul's life.

There is no specific law in the Old Testament forbidding the eating of meat sacrificed to idols, but the thinking would be the meat is defiled because of the offering to another god. However, Paul knew there is only one God and one power in the universe. His knowledge of the law freed him to eat the meat. However, the Spirit let him know the ramifications of utilizing his freedom. Paul was determined not to eat meat, out of love for his brethren. This is worshipping God in the Spirit.

Since the Spirit functions through an inward enlightening and not an external uttering, we need to validate it against the written Word. If the Spirit and the Bible do not agree, follow the written scriptures. God will never go against His Word.

Worshipping the Lord in Spirit and Truth is obeying the voice of God through the written Word (Truth) and unwritten Word (Spirit). Therefore, worship, which is devotion or reverence, can be done anywhere and anytime. True worship does not need a religious component. The worship portion of our Church services is not true worship, according to what Jesus described.

Speaking in unknown tongues is not worshipping in the Spirit. The use of tongues in Church is for prophesy. Paul states, "If there is no interpreter, let them keep silent. If there is someone to interpret, no more than two or three should speak in tongues."[34] The purpose of tongues is to edify the believers or to draw unbelievers. However, the purpose of worship is to honor God. So, tongues are for the benefit of humanity and worship is for God.

Praise is not true worship either. Praise is a form of thanksgiving, which is an offering to God for what He has done in our lives or an expression of admiration to the Lord. True praise must coincide with worship in order to be accepted by God. Otherwise, it is considered vain (empty) and God considers us hypocrites.[35] True worship, which is obedience to God's Word, is better than the sacrifice of praise offerings.[36]

Think about worship this way. Where does God reside? Where is His Kingdom? Where is His temple? The answer to all of these questions is inside of us. Therefore, true worship must occur within us. It cannot be an external act. Unfortunately, a lot of people are going to Church to worship God and to seek His face. True worship is a life transformed by the Spirit and Word of God. It happens every day, not just on Sundays or Saturdays.

We are called to be spiritual Israel (the righteous of God), not a Church. The Church building is not the Kingdom and God's government is not the Church. What is the purpose of the Church? This is where the people of God assemble to hear from leadership concerning the Kingdom. We do not meet in order to enlarge the gathering place, but to build up the Kingdom. The goal should not be to construct bigger facilities, but to impact the world for good and for God.

Spiritual Israel is called to be a kingdom of priests. Somehow, we have gotten the idea that the Jews have dropped the ball and now the Church is fulfilling their call. This notion however is erroneous and very divisive. Israel means the righteousness of God and it is our (Jew and Gentile) mission to be a kingdom of priests. We are not called to replace Israel, but to join them as one people before God.

All of this may sound like semantics. You may think there is virtually no difference between spiritual Israel and the Church. Let me be clear, I am not advocating that we start calling the Church, Israel or that we should stop going to it. However, we need to see the truth of the matter and walk accordingly. This will transform the Church into God's image for it. We should strip off all meaningless traditions and hold to what is truly from God.

Salvation

Romans 10:9 That if thou shalt confess with thy mouth the Lord Jesus, and shalt believe in thine heart that God hath raised him from the dead, thou shalt be saved.
Romans 10:10 For with the heart man believeth unto righteousness; and with the mouth confession is made unto salvation.

If we take this scripture literally, then only Christians are saved. This is what the Church preaches and teaches. To suggest anything else would be to risk being stoned. Therefore, I will tread carefully.

According to this definition, is ancient Israel saved? How about those born after Jesus' resurrection, which lived faraway from Israel and never heard the Gospel, are they saved? Think about this, in America the Bible was not introduced until the British began to colonize. The Native Americans who never heard the Gospel, are they destined to go to hell? What happens to all of the people who lived and never heard of Jesus?

Salvation is not a term exclusive to the New Testament. It is used extensively in the Old Testament in connection with Israel. The word means liberation or victory from something.

Since we know the physical always precedes the spiritual, we should look at Israel to understand the term. Israel looked to God for salvation externally and internally. Periodically, they needed victory from the outside nations and at other times they needed liberation from corrupt leaders within.

The same holds true on the spiritual side. Externally, we need victory over outside forces (people and circumstances). On the inside, we need liberation from personal strongholds (habits and thoughts).

Salvation has two components, the present and eternity. The end result of our salvation is inheriting eternal life and the Kingdom of God. Jesus came to liberate us and to give us the victory in all things that pertain to this life.

> *Galatians 5:1* ***Stand fast therefore in the liberty wherewith Christ hath made us free***, *and be not entangled again with the yoke of bondage.*

This is what makes the gospel good news. Jesus has made us free, through His death on the cross. How does the death of Jesus accomplish this for us? To answer this question we need to look at Adam and the origin of sin.

God told Adam (male and female) if you eat from the tree of knowledge of good and evil, in that day you will die.[37] After they transgressed God's command, He informed them of the consequences of their sin.

> *Genesis 3:19 In the sweat of thy face shalt thou eat bread, till thou return unto the ground; for out of it wast thou taken:* ***for dust thou art, and unto dust shalt thou return.***

"This scripture talks about returning to the dust. The implication is Adam was not meant to die and death came about through the fall. However, they did not die immediately after the fruit was eaten. Genesis 5:5 shows

Adam lived a long life and died at the ripe old age of nine hundred and thirty. Therefore, physical death could not be what God meant.

The Bible declares God is the source of all life. Therefore, separation from God means death and this is what the writer of Genesis is implying. Once God fused His Spirit with our frame (dust), the result was an immortal soul. At the point of physical death, the soul of humans is supposed to return to God. This is life eternal. In Genesis 3:19, we have Adam returning to the dust. This is eternal damnation.

The pictorial illustration is humanity going down to the grave, instead of up to God. This is death, in a spiritual sense. The soul never dies. We do not just cease to exist. The Bible teaches we have either everlasting life or eternal damnation.[38] The purpose of the last Adam (Jesus) is to restore us to life eternal."[39]

Adam represents the federal head of humanity. This means what happened to him affected all of his descendants. The only way to interrupt this succession of death is to introduce another federal head, Jesus Christ. The sign of Adam's death was the removal of God's Spirit (the Tree of Life) from humanity. Conversely, the sign of restoration is the Holy Spirit given on the day of Pentecost (the Cloven Tongues).

Adam was born through the Spirit of God interacting with the created earth. Likewise, Jesus was born by the Holy Ghost overshadowing an earthen vessel, called Mary. Since, Adam and Jesus have no physical father, only they qualify to be federal heads.

If Jesus had to pay for His own sins, He could not bear our iniquities. Since Jesus was without sin, no one born through Him has sin imputed to them.

How are we born of the Spirit? To understand this spiritual principle we need to look at the natural again. In order to be born a child does not have to do anything. Birth comes about because of the action of the parents, not the children.

> *Romans 5:18* ***Therefore as by the offence of one*** *judgment [death]* ***came upon all men*** *to condemnation; even so by* ***the righteousness of one*** *the free gift [eternal life]* ***came upon all men*** *unto justification of life.*

The apostle Paul declares just as death came to all people through Adam, in the same manner eternal life is given to all, through Jesus Christ. If by one, all are condemned then by one, grace abounds (overflows) to all. This is the love of God towards us.

In the book of Ephesians Paul declares, "For by grace you are saved through faith and not of yourselves. It is the gift of God, not of works, lest any man should boast." (Ephesians 2:8-9) This means there is nothing we can do to earn salvation. If we need to believe and confess certain things, then we are in fact doing something to achieve salvation. We could boast in the fact we have done what God requires. However, this undeniably goes against the scriptures. Why then does the Bible tell us salvation is through believing and confessing?

These things are used as proof that someone has accepted (believed) and claimed (confessed) God's gift. However, the gift is yours whether you believe it or not.

Think about it this way, what did you have to do in order to be considered a sinner? The answer is absolutely nothing. So, would God be just in making everyone confess and believe to be saved? The Bible declares where sin did abound (through Adam), grace does abound much more (through Christ). If we must do something to receive grace, then its effect is less than sin not more.

The only action required by us, is rejecting the gift. In order to reject it, we must first believe (understand) and subsequently refuse the gift. This is what Paul is talking about in the book of Hebrews.

> *Hebrews 6:4* ***For it is impossible for those who were once enlightened, and have tasted of the heavenly gift, and were made partakers of the Holy Ghost,***
> *Hebrews 6:5 And have tasted the good word of God, and the powers of the world to come,*
> *Hebrews 6:6* ***If they shall fall away, to renew them again unto repentance;*** *seeing they crucify to themselves the Son of God afresh, and put him to an open shame.*

If we do not believe and confess the Lord Jesus (the Word), then we run the risk of living beneath our privilege. It is as if someone deposited a hundred million dollars in our name, at a certain bank. Then, they inform us via email of this fact, but we do not believe them. We are not really rejecting the money. No one would jump to that conclusion, because it simply is not true. If we do not believe the story we will not live as if we are rich. This would be a tragedy because the fact of the matter is we are wealthy.

The same holds true of not believing in the work of Christ. However, it only affects us in this life. God gives us authority, power and eternal life through the Holy Spirit. If we do not believe, we may not live the abundant life Jesus promised us and this would be a real tragedy. However, when we physically die, we will still have eternal life. This is one of the reasons God will wipe the tears from our eyes, because after this life we will surely regret not using everything He has given us.[40]

Jesus commissioned believers to proclaim the good news (gospel) of the Kingdom, so no one will squander the gift of God. It has nothing to do with going to hell. It is all about knowing the Truth. Once we know and understand the Truth of God, we will be free.[41] This is salvation.

Let's look at another practical application of our salvation. The thirteenth Amendment to the United States Constitution abolished slavery and involuntary servitude. This act changed the legal status of millions of blacks, from slaves to free people. Did believing the amendment make anyone free? No, the signed document is what made them free. What did believing do for slaves then? After they received the news they refused to be treated as slaves, any longer. The same is true for us in the spiritual sense, concerning salvation. Our belief system will change how we live. It is not enough to be saved, but we must live like we are saved. This is the purpose of witnessing to unbelievers.

> *St. Mark 16:15 And he said unto them,* **Go ye into all the world, and preach the gospel to every creature.**

We do not testify in order for people to obtain salvation, that is a done deal. We witness to others in order for them to understand the free gift they have been given. So, they can live life in a more abundant manner, the way God has ordained for us.

So to answer our question from the start of the chapter, "What happens to all of the people who lived and never heard of Jesus?" God in His infinite wisdom and love has provided salvation to all people. Salvation is not exclusive to the Church, but it is inclusive to all people. This is why the gospel of Jesus is truly good news.

Church Leadership

Genesis 3:16 Unto the woman he said, I will greatly multiply thy sorrow and thy conception; in sorrow thou shalt bring forth children; and thy desire shall be to thy husband, and he shall rule over thee.

In order to understand the place of religion in our lives we should start at the beginning. We do not normally connect Genesis 3:16 with religion, but with a punishment related to the female entity called Eve.

We saw earlier the Woman represents the Holy City of God. In the Old Testament she would normally equate to Israel (Jerusalem) and in the New Testament she would embody the Church (New Jerusalem). This means we need to reexamine the story of Eden. However, that is beyond the scope of this book.

God told the Woman her desire will be to her husband and he will rule over her. Remember, this is a curse not a blessing or the norm. Since, the Woman is not an actual female, what is the writer trying to convey to us?

The Woman or city symbolizes God's people. They will long for their husband, and this husband will rule over them.

Who is the husband? In the story, Adam is the husband. Remember, Adam represents both the male and female. Therefore, the husband represents the head of the human race. The writer is telling us due to their sin or sin nature God's people will desire human leadership over God's authority. We see the truth of this played out in the book of First Samuel.

> *1 Samuel 8:6   But the thing displeased Samuel, when they said,* **Give us a king to judge us.** *And Samuel prayed unto the LORD.*
> *1 Samuel 8:7   And the LORD said unto Samuel, Hearken unto the voice of the people in all that they say unto thee: for* **they have not rejected thee, but they have rejected me, that I should not reign over them.**

Here we have Israel who asked Samuel to give them a king to rule, rather than God.   The Lord warned them of the consequences of this action, but they chose human leadership anyway.   Up until this point, ancient Israel was a theocracy, not a monarchy.

Jesus restored all things.   He sits as sovereign over the Kingdom forever.   This would lead us to believe His government is a monarchy, but it is not.   Since, He is not physically ruling on earth, it is a theocracy.   Leaders function as judges and teachers over the people of God.

> *St. Mark 10:42   But* **Jesus called them to him, and saith unto them, Ye know that they which are accounted to rule over the Gentiles exercise lordship over them;** *and their great ones exercise authority upon them.*
> *St. Mark 10:43*   **But so shall it not be among you:** *but* **whosoever will be great among you, shall be your minister:**
> *St. Mark 10:44   And* **whosoever of you will be the chiefest, shall be servant of all.**

St. Mark 10:45 For even the Son of man came not to be ministered unto, but to minister, and to give his life a ransom for many.

According to Jesus, no leader in the Church is supposed to lord over anyone else, but rather they become servants to the congregation. He washed the feet of His disciples as an example of this principle, which is one of the lowest servant jobs in the house. Religious leaders of His time would never do such a thing. Unfortunately, we would be hard pressed today to find pastors, bishops, apostles and the like doing anything remotely similar.

Jesus explicitly laid out how leadership should function in the Church. However, she (God's people) still desires to be ruled by her husband. Consequently, we have elevated leadership from servanthood to semi-divine figures.

Religious leaders are believed to have a special personal relationship with God. We have taken an Old Testament paradigm and wrongly carried it forward to the Church age. For example, God spoke with Moses directly, but not with the congregation. Moses was the mouthpiece of God, because the Spirit rested on him.

*1 John 2:27 But **the anointing which ye have received of him abideth in you, and ye need not that any man teach you**: but as the same anointing teacheth you of all things, and is truth, and is no lie, and even as it hath taught you, ye shall abide in him.*

The Spirit of God has been poured out on all flesh (people). This means the Lord speaks to everyone freely through His Spirit. There is no longer a designated few. In the garden God came to Adam and the Woman in the cool of the day.[42] This would include the whole congregation, not just leadership.

The Church today fills only the religious component of the Kingdom of God. However, this is not God's intention. The Church is meant to be the outward expression of the inner reality of God's Kingdom.

The Kingdom is a governmental body (body of Christ) invested with the authority to make decisions within any political system.

What is the purpose of government? There is no one answer, but most will agree the basic role of government is to protect its citizens. In other words, government protects our life, liberty and pursuit of happiness.

Since the Kingdom of God is spiritual, how is this accomplished? When we understand and exercise our rights, we insure we are living the way God intended.

> *2 Timothy 3:16* **All scripture** *is given by inspiration of God, and* **is profitable for doctrine, for reproof, for correction, for instruction in righteousness***:*
> *2 Timothy 3:17* **That the man of God may be perfect [mature]***, throughly furnished unto all good works.*

Jesus put it this way, "I came so that you would have life and have it more abundantly."[43] In plain English, Jesus came so we could experience this life to its fullest. This cannot be accomplished through praise and worship, offerings or anything else done within the confines of the building we call the Church.

These principles should be taught and expounded upon in Church. The acts that will cause us to experience abundant life are done outside of the building. We are meant to experience the truth and it will make us free.[44]

This means Christians should be the happiest, most fulfilled people on the planet, because we have tapped into the abundant life. Unfortunately, this is not the case at all.

"Abundant life is our heritage and our calling, but in order to live abundantly we must first understand what it entails and second we must have goals. The Lord will enable us to succeed, but we still have to have the vision, drive and action to make it happen."[45]

Proverbs 29:18 **Where there is no vision, the people perish:**

We normally associate this scripture with the Church and consequently, we believe the vision belongs to the Pastor. However, this scripture also applies to the people of God. Unfortunately, we normally do not talk about that aspect of it. If we are going to live the abundant life, we must have a vision.

People do not physically die without have a vision or goal. Instead, they languish. In other words, they become the walking dead, stuck in a religious rut. God does not want us simply going through the motions. He wants us to be fervent (red hot) in our Christian walk.

Everyone needs a personal vision for their life. It does not have to be spiritual or religious in nature, because whatever you do in life should give glory to God. Dream big and pursue what is in your heart. The book of Proverbs reveals that hope deferred makes the heart sick.[46] So do not put your dreams off. Jesus said, "Ask and you will receive that your joy may be made full."[47]

When we apply the vision solely to the Church, it becomes something to be served. This means we now serve leadership, instead of it serving us. We heap praise, money and fame upon those in leadership and justify it by saying, "A laborer is worthy of his hire."[48] We forget, God is the householder that hires the laborers and He will pay us at the end of our lives.[49]

Jesus said if we want to lead, then we must serve. Heading the Church, project or ministry is not necessarily serving. Christ tied a towel around His waist and washed His followers' feet. This was the lowest job in the house. Should leaders start washing everyone's feet? God forbid that would surely miss the point.

Leadership should be working side by side with the congregation on a regular basis. Leading by example, doing whatever needs to be done.

Today the mindset of leadership seems to be I did all of that years ago and now it is my time to be served. It is as if being served is the reward for all your earlier labor. However, this is in direct opposition to what Jesus taught.

If your local Church is not functioning according to the model of leadership Jesus prescribed, then it has displaced the Kingdom model and you are probably serving your husband (human leadership), under the guise of serving God.

In the Church world, many leaders still use the shepherd and sheep analogy. The problem is this metaphor should have ended on the day of Pentecost. The analogy stems from the fact that in the Old Testament era, God spoke to the leaders of Israel and they in turn spoke to the congregation. Therefore, if the average person needed God's direction on any matter, they had to depend on a prophet or leader. However, this process ended with the outpouring of the Holy Ghost. Now all believers have access to God directly via the Holy Spirit.

I have witnessed many churches where the mentality seems to be the pastor is the shepherd and the congregation is the sheep. On the surface this seems okay, but when you delve into it you begin to see the problems.

The shepherd and sheep analogy is correct when God is the shepherd. However, we need to be cautious when applying this to human leadership. This paradigm has been employed by the Church to control people. I have observed members getting permission to get married or even to move out of state.

We do not need a leader to help navigate us through every phase of life. A pastor is called to be our spiritual leader, not our parent. Jesus said, "I send you forth as sheep in the midst of wolves: be therefore wise as serpents and harmless as doves."[50] We must be on guard against allowing those over us, to manipulate and exploit us.

There are scriptures that state, "we should count elders that rule well of double honor and we should never muzzle the ox that treads the corn."[51] However, Paul also said, "he preached the gospel without charge, so that he did not abuse his power (1 Corinthians 9:18)."[52] We should be on guard against being manipulated into giving. Is giving to the leader something that flows from the congregation or is it compulsory? Is giving to your leader a surprise or is it expected and/or demanded?

Jesus not only gave us an object lesson on true leadership by washing His disciples' feet, but He also illustrated it through parable.

> *St. Luke 17:7 But **which of you, having a servant plowing or feeding cattle, will say unto him by and by, when he is come from the field, Go and sit down to meat?***
> *St. Luke 17:8 And **will not rather say unto him, Make ready wherewith I may sup, and gird thyself, and serve me**, till I have eaten and drunken; and afterward thou shalt eat and drink?*
> *St. Luke 17:9 **Doth he thank that servant because he did the things that were commanded him?** I trow not.*
> *St. Luke 17:10 **So likewise ye, when ye shall have done all those things which are commanded you, say, We are unprofitable servants: we have done that which was our duty to do**.*

This is the attitude of servanthood that God desires. I believe this parable is especially for leaders of God's people. It reminds us to be humble, because sometimes we get caught up in our gifts and abilities and we actually think we are special. God uses us not because we are great, but it is just the opposite. When He uses us, people will see the power is truly of God and not us.

The Sabbath

Exodus 20:8 Remember the sabbath day, to keep it holy.
Exodus 20:9 Six days shalt thou labour, and do all thy work:
Exodus 20:10 But the seventh day *is* the sabbath of the LORD thy God: *in it* thou shalt not do any work, thou, nor thy son, nor thy daughter, thy manservant, nor thy maidservant, nor thy cattle, nor thy stranger that *is* within thy gates:
Exodus 20:11 For *in* six days the LORD made heaven and earth, the sea, and all that in them *is*, and rested the seventh day: wherefore the LORD blessed the sabbath day, and hallowed it.

Remember the Sabbath and keep it holy. The Sabbath is on Saturday. However, most Christians observe Sunday as a day of worship and rest. The Sabbath versus Sunday debate was so intense in the first centuries, thousands were tortured and put to death over it. Sadly, today the controversy still rages causing a schism in the Church.

There should be no dispute over the fact that Saturday is the Sabbath of the Bible. Nevertheless, Christianity eventually came to view Sunday as the "Christian Sabbath." The prevailing position in Western Christianity is that observance of the Lord's Day, which is Sunday, replaced the Jewish Sabbath. The reasoning for this is the Lord's Day celebrated the resurrection of Jesus and the Christian's subsequent deliverance from sin. Early Christians observed the Sabbath and gathered on the first day. But, by the 4th century, Christians were officially observing, Sunday as their day of rest, and not the Sabbath.

Why did the Church switch days? The Roman Empire had a growing hostility with the Jews. After Rome adopted Christianity as their state religion, they wanted to differentiate themselves from Judaism.

The Edict of Constantine 321 A.D. stated, "On the venerable day of the Sun let the magistrates and people residing in the cities rest, and let all workshops be closed." Sunday is the day of the Sun, the name of the first day of the week, is derived from Hellenistic astrology. Sun worship can be found throughout most of recorded history in various forms, because of its perceived power and strength. However, despite the decree, Christians still observed the Sabbath.

> **Synod of Laodicea - Canon 29 A.D. 343-381**
> "CHRISTIANS must not Judaize by resting on the Sabbath, but must work on that day, rather honouring the Lord's Day; and, if they can, resting then as Christians. But if any shall be found to be Judaizers, let them be anathema from Christ."

The Empire took a stronger stance and made it unchristian to rest on Saturday. This canon basically made observing the Sabbath strictly a Jewish custom and anyone who followed it cursed (Anathema) by God.

Honoring Sunday as a day of rest derives from pagan practices. But, the same is true for all the days of the week and almost every Christian holiday we celebrate today.

Observing Sunday as a day of worship and rest is not the real problem. The issue is what we do on Saturday. Is it a sin to not observe the actual Sabbath? This question must be answered.

Sabbatarians (Sabbath keepers) claim those who do not observe the Sabbath will almost always cite three passages they interpret as Paul relieving us from the Sabbath rest. Therefore, we should review these scriptures.

1. Colossians 2:16, 17
2. Romans 14:5
3. Galatians 4:9&10

Let's look at Colossians first. The contention is that Paul is saying the Law has been abolished.

> *Colossians 2:16* ***Let no man therefore judge you*** *in meat, or in drink, or* ***in respect of*** *an holyday, or of the new moon, or of* ***the sabbath days****:*
> *Colossians 2:17 Which are a shadow of things to come; but the body is of Christ.*

The apostle Paul is sending this letter to the Church at Colossae. The Church is Gentile, not Jewish. Paul is warning the Church not to allow the Jews to make them feel condemned in relation to observing their customs. If the Sabbath is a requirement, why is Paul telling this Church not to feel judged?

> *Colossians 2:20* ***Wherefore if ye be dead with Christ*** *from the rudiments of the world,* ***why, as though living in the world, are ye subject to ordinances,***
> *Colossians 2:21 (Touch not; taste not; handle not;*
> *Colossians 2:22 Which all are to perish with the using;)* ***after the commandments and doctrines of men?***

Paul is not claiming the Law has been abolished, but that we are considered dead in Christ and are therefore exempt from the Law. The reasoning being the Law only pertains to the living, not the dead. So, according to Paul, the Church of Colossae is exempt from the decrees. It states, we are released from the commandment and doctrines of men. But, the Sabbath mandate comes directly from God, not man. So, this passage is inconclusive concerning the Sabbath. Let's look at Romans to see if it sheds more light on the subject.

> *Romans 14:5* **One man esteemeth one day above another: another esteemeth every day alike. Let every man be fully persuaded in his own mind.**
> *Romans 14:6* **He that regardeth the day, regardeth it unto the Lord; and he that regardeth not the day, to the Lord he doth not regard it.** *He that eateth, eateth to the Lord, for he giveth God thanks; and he that eateth not, to the Lord he eateth not, and giveth God thanks.*

The apostle Paul is sending this letter to the Church at Rome. This Church is also Gentile. Paul is again warning the Church not to allow the Jews to make them feel condemned in relation to observing their customs.

Sabbath keepers argue Paul was talking about fasting days, not the Sabbath. They contend if he were going to do away with one of God's Ten Commandments, he would have used less ambiguous language. It is therefore unreasonable not to honor the Sabbath.

If we look at the verses in isolation, I agree Paul could be talking about fast days. However, if we look at the whole context of what Paul is writing, it looks like he is referring to the Sabbath. In order to get the whole context, we must look at the preceding chapter. Note, chapter divisions in our Bible were not in the original manuscripts, but were added around 1,200 AD. Although usually well done, sometimes the chapter divisions interrupt the natural flow of the text.

Just before Paul goes into his topic about observing days and fasting, he talks about the Law, specifically the Ten Commandments.

> *Romans 13:8* **Owe no man any thing, but to love one another:** *for he that loveth another hath fulfilled the law.*
> *Romans 13:9* **For this**, *Thou shalt not commit adultery, Thou shalt not kill, Thou shalt not steal, Thou shalt not bear false witness, Thou shalt not covet;* **and if there be any other commandment**, *it* **is briefly comprehended in this saying, namely, Thou shalt love thy neighbour as thyself.**
> *Romans 13:10* *Love worketh no ill to his neighbour:* **therefore love is the fulfilling of the law.**

Once again, Paul is not claiming the Law has been abolished, but if we love, then we are fulfilling it. The Pharisees asked Jesus, "Which is the great commandment in the Law?"[53] He responded, "Thou shalt love the Lord thy God with all thy heart, and with all thy soul, and with all thy mind. This is the first and great commandment. And the second is like unto it, Thou shalt love thy neighbor as thyself. On these two hang all the law and the prophets."[54]

In other words, Jesus is saying the first four commandments are grouped under love of God and the last six are under loving our neighbor. Therefore, Paul is correct in saying he that loves another has satisfied the Law.

Romans chapter thirteen seems to be talking specifically about loving our neighbor, but there is no mention of God. The question becomes, how do we love God?

> *1 John 4:20* **If a man say, I love God, and hateth his brother, he is a liar:** *for he that loveth not his brother whom he hath seen, how can he love God whom he hath not seen?*
> *1 John 4:21 And this commandment have we from him, That* **he who loveth God love his brother also**.

The book of 1 John declares the only way we can truly love God is by loving our brethren. Therefore, when we love our neighbor we prove our love to God.

What does Jesus mean when he says, "All of the Law and prophets hang on loving God and loving our neighbor?" Love is the objective of the entire Law and the reason for the prophetic words. Love is the intention of the commandments. Every command is meant to bring us to this realization. If we believe we can honor God by keeping the Sabbath, then we have missed the whole point of the Law.

Let's look at the last passage normally used to support not keeping the Sabbath.

> *Galatians 4:9 But* **now, after that ye have known God**, *or rather are known of God, how turn ye again to the weak and beggarly elements, whereunto* **ye desire again to be in bondage?**
> *Galatians 4:10 Ye observe days, and months, and times, and years.*

The apostle Paul is sending this letter to the Church at Galatia. Once again, this Church is Gentile and Paul is warning them not to allow the Jews to make them feel condemned in relation to observing their customs.

If we look at the verses in isolation, I could believe Paul could be talking about pagan observances. Again, we must look at the whole context of what Paul is writing he is referring to the Law.

The argument here is Paul cannot possibly be referring to the Law, because by his own admission the Law is holy, just and good.[55] So, the bondage mentioned in verse nine cannot refer to commandments of God. That sounds right, but is this true?

We must read the whole chapter in order to get the context of what Paul is saying and then we can identify the desire, which will place them in bondage again.

> Galatians 4:21 **Tell me, ye that desire to be under the law**, do ye not hear the law?

Adherence to the Law is what they desire. This comes from the influence of the Jews. In verse seventeen he says, "They zealously affect you, but not well [for good]." So, Paul is telling us again, we are no longer under the Law.

We still need to answer the question, is the Law bondage? To answer this question correctly, we must understand what is meant by the term, from a biblical perspective. In Israel when someone cannot pay their debt, they are sold into bondage to the creditor until the obligation is paid. The penalty for breaking the Law is death, which is eternal separation from God (damnation). Biblically speaking we have all been sold unto sin through Adam. "The sting of death is sin and the strength of sin is the Law." If the Law did not exist, then sin could not be charged to us and we would have no debt. The reality is the Law does exist. Therefore, we are in bondage because of the Law.

> *Galatians 5:2* **Behold, I Paul say unto you,** *that if ye be circumcised, Christ shall profit you nothing.*
> *Galatians 5:3* *For I testify again to* **every man that is circumcised, that he is a debtor to do the whole law.**
> *Galatians 5:4* *Christ is become of no effect unto you,* **whosoever of you are justified by the law; ye are fallen from grace.**
> *Galatians 5:5* *For we through the Spirit wait for the hope of righteousness by faith.*
> *Galatians 5:6* **For in Jesus Christ neither circumcision availeth anything, nor uncircumcision; but faith which worketh by love.**

If we keep the Sabbath because we believe it is a sin not to observe it. We are unwittingly placing ourselves back under the bondage of the Law and have fallen from grace. Through Christ we have been redeemed from the Law and are now under the Spirit of Grace.[56] The law of grace is love, which is the fulfillment of the Mosaic Law.

I believe all three passages we have reviewed indicate believers do not have to observe the Sabbath. Does this mean we are free to break the commandments of God? Of course not, we are called to be a holy people.

We are freed from the Mosaic Law by the death of Jesus and now we follow the law of the Spirit, written upon our hearts. The law of the Spirit is love. All of the commandments and the prophets direct us to love our neighbor. Showing love to our neighbor is proof that we love God.

Let's look at two more passages before we make a final decision about this subject.

1. St. John 13:34
2. Acts 15:22-29

As we saw earlier, Jesus is the prophet God raised up like unto Moses. Moses is recognized as the Law giver. In order for Jesus to be like him, he must also give us God's Law.

> *St. John 13:34* ***A new commandment*** *I give unto you, That ye* ***love one another; as I have loved you***, *that ye also love one another.*

Jesus gave his disciples a new commandment. This means one of two things, either this is an addition to the Mosaic Law or it supersedes it. Since we know Christ freed us from the Law of Moses, this new commandment replaces the old. If this command were in addition to what Moses gave, then we would all be under the Law. Clearly, this is not the case. This new Law is spiritual and is written on our hearts by the Holy Spirit.

Jewish law has 613 commandments, but Jesus whittled it down to just one. However, He did not stop there, Jesus eliminated the loophole. The second greatest command is to love your neighbor as yourself. The golden rule is built from this commandment. However, you only have to love someone as much as you do yourself. What happens if you do not love yourself?

Jesus the Law Giver has eliminated this loophole. His command pushes us to love others, as He has loved us. Jesus loved us so much He gave His life, for ours. This is what I dub the platinum rule.

The next passage looks at what the council of apostles thought about Gentile converts following the Law.

> *Acts 15:22 Then pleased it **the apostles and elders, with the whole Church, to send chosen men of their own company to Antioch with Paul and Barnabas;** namely, Judas surnamed Barsabas, and Silas, chief men among the brethren:*
> *Acts 15:23 **And they wrote letters by them after this manner;** The apostles and elders and brethren send greeting unto the brethren which are of the Gentiles in Antioch and Syria and Cilicia:*
> *Acts 15:24 Forasmuch as **we have heard, that certain which went out from us have troubled you** with words, subverting your souls, **saying, Ye must be circumcised, and keep the law: to whom we gave no such commandment:***

In this passage, we have Jews troubling Gentile converts once again. This theme has been running through all of the texts we reviewed. The Jews are telling the Gentiles they must be circumcised and follow the Law. However, the apostles, elders, the whole Church and the Holy Ghost ruled against mandating circumcision and following the Law.

> *Acts 15:28 **For it seemed good to the Holy Ghost, and to us**, to lay upon you no greater burden than these necessary things;*
> *Acts 15:29 **That ye abstain from meats offered to idols, and from blood, and from things strangled,***

and from fornication: from which if ye keep yourselves, ye shall do well. Fare ye well.

The official statement from the Church, (apostles and elders) which was predominately Jewish at the time did not require us to follow the Law. Yet, almost two thousand years later we are still trying to adhere to pieces of it.

There are many more instances in scripture that admonish us to follow the Spirit (Law written on our hearts), not the letter (Law of Moses). We are no longer under the Law, due to the work of Christ on the cross. This does not mean we are lawless. To the contrary we obey a higher law, the Law of the Spirit.

We have splintered Churches and formed whole religions based on this one command. Whether we worship on Saturday or Sunday, we are required to walk in love. Therefore, we cannot stand in judgement or condemn the belief of others concerning the Sabbath and claim we are following God.

*St Mark 2:27 And he said unto them, **The sabbath was made for man, and not man for the sabbath**:*
St Mark 2:28 Therefore the Son of man is Lord also of the sabbath.

We need to do more than know the commandments. We need to understand the reasoning behind them. This is why Jesus stated the Sabbath was made for man and not man for the Sabbath. The Sabbath was created for the benefit of humankind. In other words, the Sabbath is meant to serve us and not the other way around. It is an ordinance designed to show us we need to rest. Constant work is counterproductive. This is the wisdom of God and it is certainly for our benefit. Hence, a period of resting is more important than a specific day.

Tithes and Offerings

Malachi 3:8 Will a man rob God? Yet ye have robbed me. But ye say, Wherein have we robbed thee? In tithes and offerings.

Malachi 3:9 Ye *are* cursed with a curse: for ye have robbed me, *even* this whole nation.

Malachi 3:10 Bring ye all the tithes into the storehouse, that there may be meat in mine house, and prove me now herewith, saith the LORD of hosts, if I will not open you the windows of heaven, and pour you out a blessing, that *there shall* not *be room* enough *to receive it.*

Malachi 3:11 And I will rebuke the devourer for your sakes, and he shall not destroy the fruits of your ground; neither shall your vine cast her fruit before the time in the field, saith the LORD of hosts.

First we will look at tithes and then offerings, because the two are not the same. In a very broad sense tithes are compulsory and offerings are voluntary. The term tithe is derived from Old English meaning ten.

There is a great deal of debate over whether or not Christians are required to tithe or not. The typical response to that question is found in Malachi chapter three. Not paying tithes is equated to robbing God and therefore it is considered a sin. The dispute stems from the fact there is no specific command to tithe by Jesus or any of the New Testament writers.

The command to tithe comes from the Mosaic Law and falls under the Old Testament dispensation. We are no longer under the Law, but have been freed from it by Christ. Why does tithing still exist today?

The support for tithing in the New Testament dispensation is anchored in the book of Hebrews.

> *Hebrews 6:1* **For this Melchisedec, king of Salem, priest of the most high God**, *who met Abraham returning from the slaughter of the kings, and blessed him;*
> *Hebrews 6:2* **To whom also Abraham gave a tenth part of all; first being by interpretation King of righteousness, and after that also King of Salem, which is, King of peace;**
> *Hebrews 6:3* *Without father, without mother, without descent, having neither beginning of days, nor end of life; but made like unto the Son of God; abideth a priest continually.*
> *Hebrews 6:4* **Now consider how great this man was, unto whom even the patriarch Abraham gave the tenth of the spoils.**
> *Hebrews 6:5* **And verily they that are of the sons of Levi, who receive the office of the priesthood, have a commandment to take tithes of the people according to the law, that is, of their brethren, though they come out of the loins of Abraham:**
> *Hebrews 6:6* *But he whose descent is not counted from them received tithes of Abraham, and blessed him that had the promises.*
> *Hebrews 6:7* *And* **without all contradiction the less is blessed of the better.**
> *Hebrews 6:8* *And here men that die receive tithes; but there he receiveth them, of whom it is witnessed that he liveth.*
> *Hebrews 6:9* *And as* **I may so say, Levi also, who receiveth tithes, payed tithes in Abraham.**

Hebrews 6:10 **For he was yet in the loins of his father, when Melchisedec met him.**

In essence, paying tithes in the new dispensation is justified by being in effect before the Law was instituted via Abraham. The premise being since tithing existed before the commandment of Moses, the abolishment of the Law cannot affect it. This is the main premise for tithing today, but does this argument hold water?

First, to be clear the Law has never been abolished. Jesus plainly stated, "Think not that I am come to destroy the law, or the prophets: I am not come to destroy, but to fulfil. For verily I say unto you, till heaven and earth pass, one jot or one tittle shall in no wise pass from the law, till all be fulfilled."[57]

The apostle Paul clears up the matter in the book of Romans the seventh chapter. He uses the analogy of death and states we are dead to the law through Christ. In this way the law has no more dominion over us. We then being dead with Christ are free from the Law.

The question still remains, since we are free from the Law are we freed from tithing? Let's look a little closer at argument.

Abraham was never commanded to pay tithes to Melchizedek king of Salem. The commandment was enacted by Moses. This in and of itself does not free us from paying tithes.

Let's turn our attention to circumcision for a moment. Abraham is commanded by God to cut the foreskin of his flesh and every male born, at the age of eight days. This practice was an everlasting covenant between God and

Abraham's seed. Years later, Moses commanded Israel to circumcise every male on the eight day, even on the Sabbath.[58]

The early Church faced the circumcision question with the Gentiles. There was a fierce debate over whether someone could be saved without being circumcised? Today the question seems absurd, but then it was a hot topic. The Church's final ruling was it is not necessary to be circumcised (Acts 15:1-30). This applies to all in the Church, Jews and Gentiles. Paul makes it plainer and renders circumcision null.

> *1 Corinthians 7:17 But **as God hath distributed to every man, as the Lord hath called every one, so let him walk. And so ordain I in all Churches.***
> *1 Corinthians 7:18 Is any man called being circumcised? let him not become uncircumcised. Is any called in uncircumcision? let him not be circumcised.*
> *1 Corinthians 7:19 **Circumcision is nothing, and uncircumcision is nothing**, but the keeping of the commandments of God.*

Since, we are not required to be circumcised, even though it was commanded by God to Abraham, before the decree of Moses. Then we cannot possibly be required to pay tithes, which were never commanded by God before the Law.

If the Church must pay tithes because Abraham did it before the Law, then we must also follow his example of circumcision. We cannot have one and not the other. The elders have ruled the Church does not have to adhere to circumcision, which God directly commanded Abraham. Then how could it be possible that we would have to observe tithing, which was never a directive of God to Abraham?

Furthermore, there is no indication or record of the early Church requiring its adherents to tithe. In fact, tithing does not become an official practice until the formation of the Roman Catholic Church.

So, how would the Church survive in today's culture? The Church is meant to thrive through the freewill offerings of believers.

> *2 Corinthians 9:6 But this I say, He which soweth sparingly shall reap also sparingly; and he which soweth bountifully shall reap also bountifully.*
> *2 Corinthians 9:7* ***Every man according as he purposeth in his heart, so let him give; not grudgingly, or of necessity****: for God loveth a cheerful giver.*

Remember what I stated in the beginning of the chapter, tithes are compulsory and offerings are voluntary. Paul told the Church of Corinth, not to give out of necessity.

How much we give is totally up to us. We can give as much or as little as we want. The key is we reap in direct proportion to what we sow. If we give sparingly, then we reap sparsely and vice versa.

Why is this true? "There is one fundamental law that governs the world. It is the law of reciprocity. Every living thing on the planet adheres to the law of sowing and reaping, without exception. Reciprocity is the law for all life on this planet, including humans.

This law did not come down from Mount Sinai with Moses, but it is just as important to us, if not more. Universal laws are invariable facts of the physical world. God put these laws into place at the inception of creation for our benefit."[59]

"The law of gravity is not a commandment like *thou shalt not kill,* or a legislative ruling like pay taxes. The latter two are written by man. They can be changed while the Law of Life is written in the fabric of the universe and cannot be broken.

Reciprocity in the Bible is known as sowing and reaping or seedtime and harvest. It is a universal law. Give and you will receive. It is not a matter of faith in God. You do not have to believe in Him to make it work. Just like the universal law of gravity causes objects with mass to fall to the ground when dropped, it applies to everything on earth. Sowing causes you to reap, unfailingly. If you want to experience the fullest of life, you must adhere to this one vital law.

The law of reciprocity is always in force. If we accept the fact that this law works, then we can use it to generate what we need. The principle of reciprocity is summed up in the golden rule.

> *St. Matthew 7:12 Therefore all things **whatsoever ye would that men should do to you, do ye even so to them:** for this is the law and the prophets.*

Jesus stated that reciprocity is the sum of the law and the prophets. In other words, the whole Old Testament is based on and can be condensed into this single decree."[60]

However, when we give our tithes or offerings in Church are we planting a seed? Many preachers will tell you when you give tithes and offerings to the Lord; you are in essence sowing seed into the Kingdom. They will tell you, this is God's divine plan to bless you and if you are not prospering this could be the reason why.

Let me be clear, putting your money in the collection plate is not a form of planting. This is not how God intended for you to build wealth.

Hear me out. I know that sounds like blasphemy. However, look at what the Word says about it.

> *Deutronomy 14:22* **Thou shalt** *truly* **tithe** *all* **the increase of thy seed,** *that the field bringeth forth year by year.*

The Law (first five books of the Bible) states we tithe the increase of our seed, not our seed. This is the produce or harvest (increase) from our seed. So, tithes and offerings are produce (fruit) that we give to God, not seeds we plant. Why is this important? Farmers do not plant fruit in the ground, but seeds. We do not confuse these things in the natural and we should not in the spiritual.

God is not blessing us because we are giving Him our fruit. He is blessing our obedience to Him. Look at what happens after we give our tithes (Malachi 3:8-12). God pours out a blessing so abundant that we will not be able to contain it all. How will He accomplish this feat? God says He will stop the devourer from destroying the fruit of our ground and from having premature fruit. Insect infestations cause's fruit to be premature, so God is saying He will stop the devourer from ruining our next harvest. Why is this significant?

Here is the problem. If you mistakenly think your tithes and offerings are seeds you have planted, then you will naturally wait for God to give the increase. Conversely, the Lord will be waiting for you to plant more seeds, so He can bless your next harvest. This is a spiritual stalemate. Nobody wins.

How does this work out in practical terms? If you are working a nine to five job, for minimum wage and paying your tithes and offerings faithfully, you naturally expect God to bless you. However you have not given Him anything to work with so, at best, you will be a blessed minimum wage earner, but you will certainly not be wealthy.

What you really want to do is to plant a seed that God can bless, in order to significantly increase you. If you stay at your minimum-wage job, then your seed could take the form of applying for and taking advantage of promotional opportunities. It could take the form of investing in stocks, bonds or real estate. It might come from making a hobby a second career or possibly from patenting a new invention, etcetera. These are examples of seeds that God can bless. But, note that He is not blessing (multiplying) what you put in the offering plate.

If we just continue to work at our same nine to five without doing anything else, we will never see real abundance. God is not at fault here, because He will be powerless to bless us.

I know there are some who declare they have received unexpected checks in the mail, due to their giving. I do not deny that God does move this way sometimes, but it is the exception rather than the rule. The fact remains nine times out of ten, you will need to plant a seed instead of waiting by the mailbox. Jesus instructed us to be wise like serpents, but as harmless as doves (St. Matthew 10:16).

The book of 2 Kings Chapter four is an excellent illustration of the seed principle. The story concerns a widow whose husband was a faithful prophet with Elisha. She was left in debt and the creditors were about to take her sons as payment. It is important to note in the story, God did not bless her tithes and offerings. He looked for and blessed what she had left, a pot of oil. The oil became her seed and she reaped enough to pay all her debts and live on the rest.[61] If we are not planting (investing) a portion of what we have left, how can God bless us?"[62]

In the early Church most leaders shunned tithing and some like Paul even refused to preach or teach for money.

> *2 Peter 2:1 But **there were false prophets also among the people, even as there shall be false teachers among you**, who privily shall bring in damnable heresies, even denying the Lord that bought them, and bring upon themselves swift destruction.*
> *2 Peter 2:2 And many shall follow their pernicious ways; by reason of whom the way of truth shall be evil spoken of.*
> *2 Peter 2:3 And through covetousness shall **they with feigned words make merchandise of you:** whose judgment now of a long time lingereth not, and their damnation slumbereth not.*

In a nutshell tithing has been eliminated. In actuality, there were three different or types of tithes in Israel. It is important to note tithing in the beginning was done with agriculture and livestock, not with money. They were instructed only to use money when it was too far the travel and then buy whatever you wanted to eat. This is because both the giver (tither) and receiver were meant to celebrate what God has given. It was a time of feasting and enjoying the bounty of the Lord. The tithe was meant to partake with the priesthood, not purely to provide for them *per se*.

Support of the Church should be through voluntary offerings. Believers should always give, but in a discerning manner. It is your money and whoever or whatever you give it to should be accountable.

If we use the knowledge of tithing not to give to the local Church, then it will fold and that would be catastrophic. It takes money to run a Church, this is a fact. Therefore, membership must give in proportion to sustain the edifice. However, this giving is through freewill offerings, not an obligation to tithe.

There was and still is a mindset that states we need to give our tithes and let God take care of how they are administered. This way our blessings are not hindered. However, this allows leadership to raise funds without accountability.

> *2 Peter 2:3 And **through covetousness shall they with feigned words make merchandise of you**: whose judgment now of a long time lingereth not, and their damnation slumbereth not.*

Unfortunately, there is a long history of leaders manipulating sincere congregants out of their money, by twisting the scriptures to justify their greed. We however, are admonished to walk in wisdom in all things.

Spiritual Maturity

1 Peter 2:2 As newborn babes, desire the sincere milk of the word, that ye may grow thereby:

One of the primary functions of a Pastor or Church leader is to feed believers the Word of God. This is so they will grow into mature believers. We see this paradigm all throughout life.

When we are new converts to Christianity, we are more dependent on leadership and this is natural. But, what happens when we are mature in our walk with Christ?

Do we still need to be fed (spiritually) through sermons every Sunday and some sort of bible study during the week, indefinitely? I know may leaders that would say yes, but is it really true?

From a natural standpoint, if you start off as a newborn and then mature into an adult. Do you need your parents to still feed you? If you are mentally and physically capable, then it is expected that adults feed themselves. Then why do believers need to be taught and instructed endlessly?

We can see logically this makes no sense, but what do the scriptures have to say about it? The prophet Jeremiah prophesied there would be a new archetype of instruction from the Old Testament method to the New Testament.

Jeremiah 31:31 ***Behold, the days come, saith the LORD, that I will make a new covenant with the house of Israel****, and with the house of Judah:*

Jeremiah 31:32 **Not according to the covenant that I made with their fathers in the day that I took them by the hand to bring them out of the land of Egypt;** *which my covenant they brake, although I was an husband unto them, saith the LORD:*
Jeremiah 31:33 But **this shall be the covenant that I will make with the house of Israel;** *After those days, saith the LORD,* **I will put my law in their inward parts, and write it in their hearts;** *and will be their God, and they shall be my people.*
Jeremiah 31:34 *And* **they shall teach no more every man his neighbour, and every man his brother, saying, Know the LORD**: *for they shall all know me, from the least of them unto the greatest of them, saith the LORD: for I will forgive their iniquity, and I will remember their sin no more.*

If we are dependent upon our leaders to feed us continually, then we are living in the Old Testament model. I am only talking about those who are or should be spiritually mature.

Am I taking this out of context? Is the scripture talking about something else when it says we will no longer have to teach people to know the Lord? To know the Lord implies a relationship and requires intimacy.

Perhaps Jeremiah was prophesying about something that is still in the future. Maybe this new covenant with Israel has not started yet.

1 John 2:27 *But* **the anointing which ye have received of him** *abideth in you, and* **ye need not that any man teach you**: *but as* **the same anointing teacheth you of all things**, *and is truth, and is no lie, and even as* **it hath taught you**, *ye shall abide in him.*

102

The new covenant with Israel is the New Testament, which has been ratified by the blood of Jesus. God now teaches us directly through His Spirit. After we have matured it is the Spirit of God that will teach us all things. Even as babes in Christ the Holy Spirit is there to guide us.

> *John 14:26 But **the Comforter, which is the Holy Ghost**, whom the Father will send in my name, **he shall teach you all things**, and bring all things to your remembrance, whatsoever I have said unto you.*

The Holy Spirit came to comfort believers in the physical absence of the Messiah. Jesus was God with them. The Holy Ghost was God in them. Christ did not teach His disciples everything they needed in life. This is why He told them the Comforter would teach them all things.

So, does this mean after we mature we no longer need a Pastor? No, that is not what I am saying. After we mature our relationship with our leader should change. If it does not then something is wrong. We should not remain dependent on Pastors for spiritual nourishment our whole lives. This negates the effectiveness of the New Covenant and places us back under the old model of the Law.

How do you know you are spiritually mature? I do not think there is one definitive answer. Are there a certain number of years after conversion that would serve as a barometer? If we are talking about biological maturity, a general indication is graduation from high school and/or turning eighteen. However, on the spiritual side one size does not fit all individuals. Spiritual maturity is more complex and difficult to gauge.

There are loads of spiritual maturity assessment tests you can take on the internet. I would not recommend them.
I looked at one assessment device and it turned out to be a tool to gauge your faithfulness to the Church. Unfortunately, devotion and Church attendance are traditionally used as gauges of maturity. This is a religious mindset, not necessarily a biblical one.

As with all things let's see what the Bible has to say about the matter. God uses the physical things we can see to help us understand the spiritual realities we cannot. There are of course many factors involved in spiritual development. I will attempt to minimize the process to the essentials.

Normal human physical development and maturity can be boiled down to growth, attaining a certain level of knowledge and assuming responsibilities. These three factors also relate to spiritual maturity.

Indicators of Spiritual Development:
1. Growth
2. Knowledge
3. Responsibilities

The first indicator of spiritual development is growth. Growing equates to change and change can be uncomfortable at times. It does not happen instantaneously and most of all it requires proper nourishment. All of this makes logical sense, but is it biblical?

> *1 Peter 2:2 **As newborn babes, desire the sincere milk of the word, that ye may grow thereby**:*

> *2 Timothy 3:16 **All scripture is given by inspiration of God, and is profitable** for doctrine,*

for reproof, for correction, for instruction in
righteousness:
2 Timothy 3:17 **That the man of God may be**
perfect *[mature or complete], throughly furnished*
unto all good works.

Clearly, spiritual growth is directly linked to the Word of God. It is not just hearing the Word, but adherence to it that fosters growth.

The second indicator of spiritual development is attaining a certain level of knowledge. This knowledge should be a byproduct of our faith. The more we read, study and obey the Word of God, the more we should grow in faith and increase in knowledge.

If we look at this in the natural sense, as we grow up we attend school. We continue this process of growing and education until we graduate from high school or college. Likewise, spiritually speaking we should graduate from needing milk to using meat. Once we are eating meat we are considered to be of mature or full age.

Hebrews 5:12 **For when for the time ye ought to**
be teachers, ye have need that one teach you again
which be **the first principles of the oracles of God;**
and are become such as have need of milk, and not
of strong meat.
Hebrews 5:13 **For every one that useth milk is**
unskilful in the word of righteousness: for he is a
babe.
Hebrews 5:14 **But strong meat belongeth to them**
that are of full age, *even those who by reason of*
use have their senses exercised to discern both good
and evil.

Attaining true maturity constitutes more than just a rote hearing and following of commands. It entails a true understanding of the principles of the Word.

The third and last indicator of spiritual development we will look at is responsibility. Mature individuals do not take on responsibilities because they are told to or because they have been forced to do it. They take on responsibilities voluntarily because they see the need. This is true in both the physical and spiritual realms. Responsibilities take the form of sacrifices and actions (our Christian walk).

> *1 Corinthians 8:9 But **take heed lest by any means this liberty of yours become a stumblingblock to them that are weak.***
> *1 Corinthians 8:10 For if any man see thee which hast knowledge sit at meat in the idol's temple, shall not the conscience of him which is weak be emboldened to eat those things which are offered to idols;*
> *1 Corinthians 8:11 And through thy knowledge shall the weak brother perish, for whom Christ died?*
> *1 Corinthians 8:12 But when ye sin so against the brethren, and wound their weak conscience, ye sin against Christ.*
> *1 Corinthians 8:13 **Wherefore, if meat make my brother to offend, I will eat no flesh while the world standeth, lest I make my brother to offend.***

The Apostle Paul's stand on not eating meat is the epitome of voluntary responsibility towards our brethren. As I stated in an earlier chapter, Paul knows there is only one God. Therefore, all idols must be false or non-existent, because the Lord is the only deity period. So, Paul knows he is free to eat meat offered to idols (discounted and sold in the markets). However, he is persuaded by wisdom to walk in love rather than knowledge concerning this matter. This is the type or level of spiritual maturity all Christians should reach.

> *1 Corinthians 8:1 Now as touching things offered unto idols, we know that we all have knowledge.* ***Knowledge puffeth up, but charity*** [love] ***edifieth****.*

The Bible admonishes us to become perfect, meaning mature or complete. Although the Word nourishes us and causes us to grow, spiritual knowledge is not the end goal. Paul states knowledge alone will only cause us to be proud and as the scriptures states "Pride comes before a fall".[63] All knowledge must be tempered with love, this is wisdom.

Just to reiterate the three indicators of spiritual development are "Growth", "Knowledge" and "Responsibilities". These of course are secular terms. The Bible uses a different vernacular to describe the same thing. Let's replace growth with faith, knowledge with hope and responsibility with love.

How does this work out exactly? We know spiritual growth comes from the Word of God. In addition, faith also comes from the Word. Faith precedes growth. It is the basis for salvation.

> *Hebrews 11:6 But* ***without faith it is impossible to please him: for he that cometh to God must believe that he is****, and that he is a rewarder of them that diligently seek him.*

Since faith is the starting point, what comes next? Hope comes after faith and the two are linked together. Hebrews

107

11:1 states, "Now faith is the substance of things hoped for, the evidence of things not seen". As I said earlier, knowledge (hope) should be a byproduct of our faith.

Hebrews states that faith is both substance and evidence. Substance means material. It is normally something that is tangible or concrete. Faith is also evidence. Evidence is the proof, sign, or substantiation of something. Faith is the substance and evidence of our hope.

Faith and Hope is not the same thing. Faith pertains to the present and Hope deals with the future. We have faith for the invisible things that are ours right now. In contrast, we have hope for the invisible things that are ours in the future. By the future I mean after this present age or life.

As we have already discussed love is the highest level of maturity. So, faith, hope and love are the spiritual indicators of our maturity in Christ. This corresponds with what the Apostle Paul wrote to the Corinthians.

> *1Corinthians 13:13 And now abideth **faith, hope, charity**, these three; but **the greatest of these is charity.***

This is by no means a definitive list of factors for determining spiritual maturity. These three things are the essentials as defined by Paul.

> *2 Peter 1:5 And beside this, giving all diligence, add to your **faith** virtue; and to **virtue** knowledge;*
> *2 Peter 1:6 And to **knowledge** temperance; and to **temperance** patience; and to **patience** godliness;*
> *2 Peter 1:7 And to **godliness** brotherly kindness; and to **brotherly kindness charity**.*

The Apostle Peter gives us a more comprehensive list of indicators. However, hope is missing from the list. If we look carefully we will see hope if inferred by the term patience.

> *Romans 8:25 But **if we hope** for that we see not, then do **we with patience wait for it**.*

> *Romans 15:4 For whatsoever things were written aforetime were written for our learning, that we through **patience** and comfort of the scriptures **might have hope**.*

Indicators of Spiritual Maturity

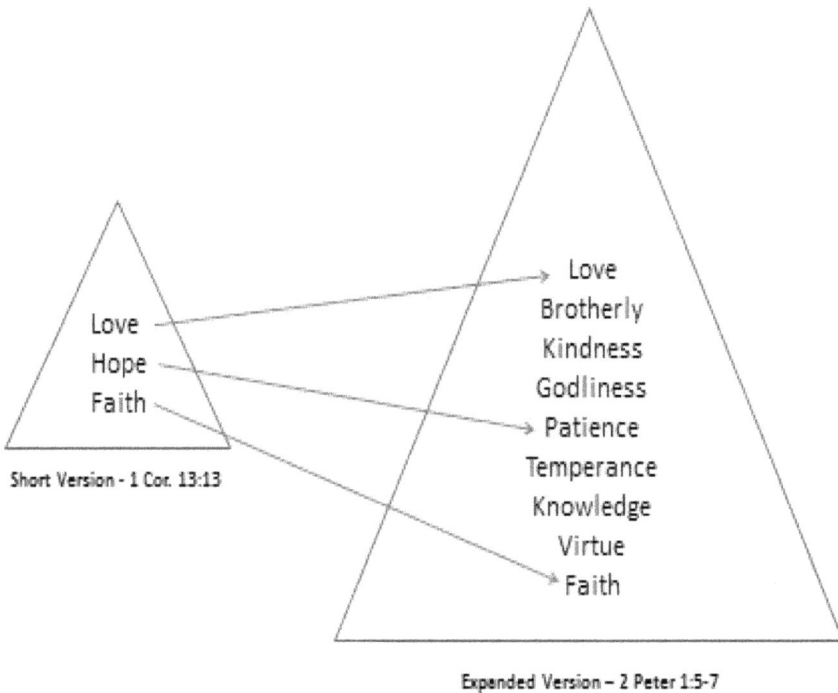

Short Version - 1 Cor. 13:13

Love
Hope
Faith

Love
Brotherly
Kindness
Godliness
Patience
Temperance
Knowledge
Virtue
Faith

Expanded Version – 2 Peter 1:5-7

So, after we mature what is our relationship to the Pastor? Are we still looking to him or her for spiritual nourishment and direction? Once a child becomes an adult there is still a relationship, but it changes. Under normal circumstances an adult is no longer dependent upon a parent. They may still get advice and guidance from time to time, but they are not reliant. Instead of requiring help, adult children provide help to their parents.

All of this holds true on the spiritual side. If this is not the case in your Church, then there are dysfunctional relationships occurring. Correcting this situation takes courage, strength and may even require healing. But, if you want the abundant life Jesus promised then things must be corrected.

What God Wants

Micah 6:6 Wherewith shall I come before the LORD, and bow myself before the high God? shall I come before him with burnt offerings, with calves of a year old?
Micah 6:7 Will the LORD be pleased with thousands of rams, or with ten thousands of rivers of oil? shall I give my firstborn for my transgression, the fruit of my body for the sin of my soul?
Micah 6:8 He hath shewed thee, O man, what is good; and what doth the LORD require of thee, but to do justly, and to love mercy, and to walk humbly with thy God?

What does God want from us? He created us in His image and gave us dominion over the earth. We sinned, so He sent His Son to redeem us. In light of all this, what does He expect from His creation?

The prophet Micah answers the question for us. God requires three things of us.

1. To do justly
2. To love mercy
3. To walk humbly with God

The first requirement is to do justly or rightly. This pertains to our individual actions. Personal conduct is directed at the self or the individual level. How do we know what is right or just? Righteousness is based on the Word of God. But, it is not a legalistic adherence to the Law.

Judgment - the act or process of forming an opinion or making a decision after careful thought

Legalism refers to any doctrine which states salvation comes strictly from adherence to the Law. It can be thought of as a works-based religion. God wants us to give careful thought to His Word and see the principle behind the commandments.

Doing justly is not simply following the Law. We must understand the aim of the command. Absolute adherence to rules tends to make us inflexible and unsympathetic towards others. Jesus took issue with the Pharisees, Sadducees and Scribes of His day for exactly this reason.

God wants our personal conduct to be based on the situation, the people involved and His Word. Since, two of the three factors are variable. Our response will not always be the same. Life is complicated and a robotic reaction is inadequate. Doing justly demands that we think, as well as act.

The Lord has entrusted us to be the gods of this world. He has given us dominion over the earth. Therefore, we must do more than follow rules. We must think and do the right thing, for the earth, the animals and each other.

Think about this, there is no biblical law prohibiting littering. But, as the custodians of the earth, should we litter? Can we do justly, if we only following the biblical commandments?

When it comes to doing the right thing we should always combine thorough reasoning with our actions. This is what it means to do justly.

The second requirement is to love mercy. This pertains to our interpersonal exchanges. In other words, how we treat each other. Let's first define mercy.

Mercy - compassion or forgiveness shown toward someone whom it is within one's power to punish or harm: kindness or help given to people who are in a distress

The definition of mercy sounds like God's character and this is how He wants His highest creation to function. This only reinforces the idea that we were made to be the gods of this world. But, why mercy, should not God require us to love each other?

It was Alexander Pope who said, "To err is human, to forgive divine." Our humanity is the crux of the matter. It is human nature to make mistakes. How many times have we said, I am only human?

Love directs us how we should act towards one another. We should treat others as we wish to be treated. But, what happens when you treat others well and they still do wrong to you? This is where mercy comes into play. I have shown you love, but still you persist in doing wrong. Now you get what you deserve, right?

It is perfectly natural to follow the eye for an eye rule, because it implies retribution. Payback is a natural reaction when someone does us wrong. The problem is summed up by the quote attributed to Gandhi, "An eye for an eye leaves the whole world blind."

A world with love and no mercy would only be favorable to us, until we make a mistake. This is not an ideal situation. It is too unforgiving and rigid. Mercy holds together the social fabric of the world.

An eye for an eye is based on the Law of Moses. It demands retribution for a wrong done. It is intended to make the punishment fit the crime. It was enacted as a means stop disproportionate reactions to offenses.

> *Exodus 21:24* **Eye for eye**, *tooth for tooth, hand for hand, foot for foot,*
> *Exodus 21:25 Burning for burning, wound for wound, stripe for stripe.*

> *Leviticus 24:20 Breach for breach,* **eye for eye,** *tooth for tooth:* **as he hath caused a blemish in a man, so shall it be done to him again.**

Conversely, mercy is based on the Law of the Spirit, which is a higher law.

> *St. Matthew 5:38* **Ye have heard that it hath been said, An eye for an eye**, *and a tooth for a tooth:*
> *St. Matthew 5:39* **But I say unto you, That ye resist not evil:** *but whosoever shall smite thee on thy right cheek, turn to him the other also.*

Here is where I believe Jesus gets a bad rap. He is not telling us to be pacifist. In fact, Jesus was considered radical and dangerous in His day and time. So, why does He tell us not to fight against those who do evil?

There is another law at play here. It is not the Law of the Spirit, nor is it the Law of love. It is the fundamental law that governs the world, the law of reciprocity. Sowing causes you to reap, unfailingly.

This is why Jesus tells us to love our enemies and to bless them that curse us.[64]   Jesus is not trying to turn us into doormats. He is trying to show us how to experience the Abundant Life God has given to all of us. If we repay people an eye for an eye, we will reap some unwanted consequences to our lives because of the principle of cause and effect.

It is important to note, sowing and reaping is not a one for one proposition. It is a one to many, relationship. The biblical definition of reaping implies a harvest. If you sow a single apple seed and it produces a tree, you will not just get one apple. Understand that God is a God of abundance. This law was set in place for our benefit, but if we sow the wrong things it could be disastrous to us. This is why God implores us to live holy and righteous lives.

The fall of man caused us to experience the bad side of reciprocity. Prior to the fall, man was sinless and only knew good. Therefore, he could never sow bad seeds nor could he reap their harvest. Once we became familiar with evil, we began to reap a harvest that set the course of humanity on fire.

After the fall, God gave us laws to realign us to receive the blessings of reciprocity."[65] This is why God tells us to love and be merciful, so we do not reap an unwanted harvest.

Love covers our interactions with each other and mercy directs us how to respond when love is not reciprocated.

The third and last requirement is to walk humbly with God. Walking is an important cultural metaphor in the world. It is a natural part of the human condition. The biblical meaning of walking with someone is symbolic with agreement.

Why does God stress that we need to walk humbly with Him? If we are doing justly and showing mercy, we must be in agreement with God, right? Just the opposite, by doing these things we are susceptible to become prideful. This is why we are admonished to be humble.

> **Pride** - a feeling or deep pleasure or satisfaction derived from one's own achievements, the achievements of those with whom one is closely associated, or from qualities or possessions that are widely admired:

The more admirable or godlike we become, the greater the propensity for pride. To experience pride is to be fully human. It is nothing to be ashamed of or to hide. Pride is useful. It can drive us to excel in life, it can eliminate mediocrity. However, it can also lead to false feelings of superiority and this is what we must be on guard against it.

Following the first two requirements of God may drive us to maintain and enhance favorable views of ourselves. The real problem with this mindset is that self-satisfaction will become our primary impetus and everything else will be subservient.

If we follow the promptings of our ego over God, then we are placing ourselves over Him. This is not our estate, in doing so we become false gods.

> *Romans 6:16* ***Know ye not, that to whom ye yield yourselves servants to obey, his servants ye are to whom ye obey;*** *whether of sin unto death, or of obedience unto righteousness?*

Jesus said, "No servant can serve two masters: for either he will hate the one and love the other; or else he will hold to the one, and despise the other."[66] The two are diametrically opposed to each other. There is no middle ground. Elijah put it this way, "How long halt you between two opinions? If the Lord be God, follow him: but if Baal, then follow him."

There is no way to walk with God in pride. The only way we can be in agreement with the Lord is through humility. Although we are the gods of this world, the Lord reigns supreme. In other words, God is the king and we are princes. If we place ourselves above the Lord, then we become false gods.

So what does God require of us? First, we must do justly. This requirement deals with the realm of self. Second, we must love mercy. This condition concerns itself with others. Last, we must walk humbly with God. This responsibility keeps our ego in perspective, so we can be like God without trying to be Him.

In the requirements there is no mention of when to worship God or how to worship Him. There is no prescription on prayer, how to or how often. Curiously, Church attendance, monetary giving, keeping the Law and any other ceremony we consider holy is noticeably missing. There is no giant list of do's and don'ts. More importantly there is nothing remotely religious listed.

There is nothing in God's requirements that should cause distinctions or divisions among people. To the contrary everything God does is unifying. Religions and denominations by their very nature divide people. Can this really be of God? The apostle Paul asked the question, "Is

Christ divided? Was Paul crucified for you? Or were you baptized in the name of Paul?"[67]

Jesus put it this way, "Every kingdom divided against itself is brought to desolation; and every city or house divided against itself shall not stand."[68] All of the fighting over and about God is not ordained by Him. The Church cannot be the Kingdom of God, look at all of the infighting within and between denominations. The book of James clearly states these things come from us, not God.[69]

The Kingdom is within us and invisible. Consequently, the Church is supposed to be the tangible representation of the power, love and mercy of God. It is the body of Christ. We have a body in order to interact with our environment, without it we cannot. Therefore, we (individually and collectively) are ordained to affect the world, in Christ's stead. What did Jesus come to do?

> *St. Luke 4:18* ***The Spirit of the Lord is upon me,*** ***because he hath anointed me*** *to* ***preach the gospel*** *to the poor; he hath sent me to* ***heal the*** ***brokenhearted,*** *to preach* ***deliverance to the*** ***captives,*** *and* ***recovering of sight to the blind,*** *to set* *at* ***liberty them that are bruised,***

"The world we live in is broken and in dire need of repair. It is filled with hunger and homelessness, poverty and pain. Inequalities exist between men and women, between the races, between the nations. Discrimination continues, despite laws that forbid it. The inhumanity of war rages despite our education and advanced culture. Crime and violence threaten our world, destroys our families and cuts short far too many lives.

Every action we take to repair the brokenness is important. Every time we volunteer at the soup kitchen, work for justice, demonstrate for a righteous cause or help make peace between individuals or nations, we are participating in the Kingdom of God.

Our actions do not always have to have grand social implications. Helping someone with a problem, saying please and thank you, smiling, showing hospitality, visiting the sick, comforting the bereaved or just being loving and kind demonstrates to the world the Kingdom has come."[70]

I read a banner next to a local church recently that summed it up perfectly. It said, "Be the Church. Protect the environment. Care for the poor. Forgive often. Reject racism. Fight for the powerless. Share earthly and spiritual resources. Embrace diversity. Love God. Enjoy this life."[71] If we do these things, it is impossible to displease God.

The myriad of doctrines, ceremonies and rules the Church requires is not what God wanted. Jesus said, "My yoke is easy and my burden is light." God asks just three practical things of us, which could easily fit in any religion or denomination. Maybe, it is time for us to rethink Church.

Robert
Your brother in Christ

About the Author

Robert R. Davis has served in a variety of ministries as a deacon, teacher, youth director, minister and Assistant Pastor. He is a gifted teacher of the Word, dedicated to pursuing and sharing the full knowledge of Christ. Robert and his wife Yvette live in Connecticut, where he continues to teach, write, and study the Word of God.

Other books written by Robert R. Davis include:

The Final Message:
Understanding the Book of Revelation

6 Things Every Christian Should Know:
The Fundamentals of Christianity

What Lies Within:
Understanding the Holy Spirit

How to Live the Abundant Life

In the Beginning:
The Truth Behind Genesis

Bibliography

[1] Holy Bible. St. Matthew 16:8

[2] The people's New Testament commentary by M. Eugene Boring, Fred B. Craddock 2004 ISBN 0-664-22754-6 page 69

[3] Papal infallibility: a Protestant evaluation of an ecumenical issue by Mark E. Powell 2009 ISBN 978-0-8028-6284-6 pages 35-40

[4] Cornel West Reader, op. cit., page 357

[5] Cornel West Reader, op. cit., page 357

[6] Rediscovering the Kingdom. Ancient Hope for our 21st Century World by Myles Munroe (Shippensburg, PA: Destiny Image Publishers Inc., 2004) ISBN 0-7684-2217-5 page 27

[7] Ibid., page 26

[8] The Adam and Eve Story: Eve Came From Where? The Biblical Archeology Society. January 2, 2017, https://www.biblicalarchaeology.org/daily/biblical-topics/bible-interpretation/the-adam-and-eve-story-eve-came-from-where/

[9] Holy Bible. Galatians 4:25-26.

[10] Holy Bible. Hebrews 12:28

[11] Holy Bible. Romans 8:18

[12] Holy Bible. St. Matthew 11:28

[13] Holy Bible. Genesis 32:24-30

[14] "Israel meaning | Israel etymology." Etymology of the name Israel. Accessed November 4, 2014, http://www.abarim-publications.com/Meaning/Israel.html#.VFkZF0oo6fA

[15] Ibid.

[16] Holy Bible. 1 Timothy 6:12

[17] "Jeshurun meaning | Jeshurun etymology." The name Jeshurun in the Bible. Accessed November , 2014, http://www.abarim-publications.com/Meaning/Jeshurun.html#.VFop8Uoo6fA

[18] Holy Bible. Genesis 26:4

[19] Holy Bible. 1 Samuel 8:4-6

[20] Holy Bible. 1 Kings 11:30-32

[21] Holy Bible. 1 Chronicles 23:25

[22] Holy Bible. St. Matthew 1:1-16

[23] Holy Bible. St. Matthew 1:20-25

[24] Holy Bible. St. Matthew 11:7-15

[25] Holy Bible. St. Mark 14:58

[26] Holy Bible. St. John 1:33

[27] The Final Message. Understanding the book of Revelation. Robert R. Davis (New Haven, CT: Kingdom Works Publishing, 2008) ISBN 978-0-9797469-0-1 pages 107

[28] Holy Bible. Galatians 3:24-25

[29] Holy Bible. Revelation 13:14-15

[30] Holy Bible. St. John 17:17

[31] Holy Bible. St. Mark 7:18

[32] Holy Bible. St. John 15:26

[33] Holy Bible. 1 Corinthians 8:13

[34] Holy Bible. 1 Corinthians 14:27-29

[35] Holy Bible. St. Matthew 15:7-9

[36] Holy Bible. 1 Samuel 15:22

[37] Holy Bible. Genesis 2:17

[38] Holy Bible. St. John 5:29

[39] In the Beginning, op. cit., pages 123-124

[40] Holy Bible. Revelation 21:4

[41] Holy Bible. St. John 8:32

[42] Holy Bible. Genesis 3:8

[43] Holy Bible. St. John 10:10

[44] Holy Bible. St. John 8:32

[45] How to live the Abundant Life. Robert R. Davis (New Haven, CT: Kingdom Works Publishing, 2011) ISBN 978-0-9797469-2-5 pages 65.

[46] Holy Bible. Proverbs 13:12.

[47] Holy Bible. St. John 16:24.

[48] Holy Bible. 1 Timothy 5:17-18

[49] Holy Bible. St. Matthew 20:1-16

[50] Holy Bible. St. Matthew 10:16

[51] Holy Bible. 1 Timothy 5:17-18

[52] Holy Bible. 1 Corinthians 9:18

[53] Holy Bible. St. Matthew 22:36

[54] Holy Bible. St. Matthew 22:37-40

[55] Holy Bible. Romans 7:12

[56] Holy Bible. Galatians 4:4-5

[57] Holy Bible. St. Matthew 5:17-18

[58] Holy Bible. St. John 7:22-23

[59] How to live the Abundant Life, op. cit., pages 9

[60] How to live the Abundant Life, op. cit., pages 9-10.

[61] Holy Bible. 2 Kings 4:1-7.

[62] How to live the Abundant Life, op. cit., pages 121-124

[63] Holy Bible. Proverbs 16:18

[64] Holy Bible. St. Matthew 5:44

[65] How to Live the Abundant Life, op. cit., page 9-15

[66] Holy Bible. St. Luke 16:13

[67] Holy Bible. 1 Corinthians 1:13

[68] Holy Bible. St. Matthew 12:25

[69] Holy Bible. James 3:17

[70] God 101. Jewish Ideals, Beliefs, and Practices for Renewing Your Faith. Rabbi Terry Bookman(New York, NY: Perigee Books, 2000) ISBN 0-399-52658-7 pages 132-134

[71] The First Church of Christ (United Church of Christ), Hartford Connecticut.

www.ingramcontent.com/pod-product-compliance
Lightning Source LLC
Chambersburg PA
CBHW071601040426
42452CB00008B/1251